THE INTERNATIONAL
POPULAR TALE
AND EARLY WELSH
TRADITION

PEIG SAYERS

THE GREGYNOG LECTURES 1961

THE INTERNATIONAL POPULAR TALE AND EARLY WELSH TRADITION

BY

Kenneth Hurlstone Jackson

M.A., LITT.D., D.LITT.CELT., F.B.A.

Professor of Celtic, Edinburgh University

CARDIFF

UNIVERSITY OF WALES PRESS

1961

PRINTED IN GREAT BRITAIN

PREFACE

THIS preface has but one purpose—the pleasant task of expressing thanks. First, to the Senate of the University College of Wales for honouring me by inviting me to deliver the Gregynog Lectures. Second, to all those friends, old and new, who made my visit to Aberystwyth such a delightful experience, particularly to my ever kind hosts Principal and Mrs. T. Parry and Professor and Mrs. T. Jones; as well as to the very responsive and encouraging audiences. Third, to the memory of those three, now all dead, named in the dedication; it would be superfluous to account for this, and let it be enough to say that without them, each in his own way, these lectures could never have been delivered.

K. H. J.

CONTENTS

ABBREVIATIONS

AT.   Antti Aarne and Stith Thompson, *The Types of the Folktale* (FFC., no. 74; Helsinki, 1928).

BDL.   Proinsias Mac Cana, *Branwen Daughter of Llyr* (Cardiff, 1958).

BP.   J. Bolte and G. Polivka, *Anmerkungen zu den Kinder- und Hausmärchen der Brüder Grimm*, 5 vols. (Leipzig, 1913–32).

CFT.   W. Eberhard, *Chinese Fairy Tales and Folk Tales* (London, 1937).

FFC.   *Folklore Fellows Communications* (Helsinki, 1907 ff.).

FHT.   J. Macdougall, *Folk and Hero Tales from Argyllshire* (*Waifs and Strays of Celtic Tradition*, Argyllshire Series, no. III; London, 1891).

GS.   J. H. Delargy, *The Gaelic Story-Teller, with Some Notes on Gaelic Folktales*; *Proceedings of the British Academy*, xxxi (1945), 177 ff. (Rhys Memorial Lecture for 1945).

IHK.   R. Thurneysen, *Irische Helden- und Königsage* (Halle, 1921).

JCS.   *The Journal of Celtic Studies.*

KS.   R. Köhler, *Kleinere Schriften zur Märchenforschung*, edited by J. Bolte; 2 vols. (Weimar, 1898–1900).

M.   G. Jones and T. Jones, *The Mabinogion* (London, Everyman Series, no. 97; 1949).

Masp.   G. Maspero, *Les Contes populaires de l'Egypte ancienne* (Paris, 1882).

MdM.   A. Wesselski, *Märchen des Mittelalters* (Berlin, 1925).

MWHT.   J. G. McKay, *More West Highland Tales*, 2 vols. (Edinburgh, 1940 and 1960).

RC.   *Revue Celtique.*

Rh.   W. J. Gruffydd, *Rhiannon, an Enquiry into the First and Third Branches of the Mabinogi* (Cardiff, 1953).

SEBC. *Studies in the Early British Church*, edited by N. K. Chadwick (Cambridge, 1958).

SHS. J. G. Campbell, *Superstitions of the Highlands and Islands of Scotland* (Glasgow, 1900).

SM. An Seabhac, *An Seanchaidhe Muimhneach* (Dublin, 1932).

ST. Stith Thompson, *Motif-Index of Folk-Literature*, 6 vols. (2nd ed., Copenhagen, 1955–8).

Tawney. C. H. Tawney, *Katha Sarit Sagara, the Ocean of the Streams of Story*; 2 vols. (Calcutta, 1880–4).

TGSI. *Transactions of the Gaelic Society of Inverness.*

TPC. T. P. Cross, *Motif-Index of Early Irish Literature* (Bloomington, Indiana, 1952).

TWH. J. F. Campbell, *Popular Tales of the West Highlands*, 4 vols. (first edition, Edinburgh 1860).

VF. C. W. von Sydow, *Våra Folksagor* (*Natur och Kultur*, no. 146; Stockholm, 1941).

VSB. A. W. Wade-Evans, *Vitae Sanctorum Britanniae et Genealogiae* (Cardiff, 1944).

VTM. A. Wesselski, *Versuch einer Theorie des Märchens* (*Prager Deutsche Studien*, no. 45, Reichenberg, 1931).

ZCP. *Zeitschrift für Celtische Philologie.*

I

The International Popular Tale: Characteristics

IN a series of articles, lectures, and books extending over many years, the origin, construction, and significance of the *Four Branches* and some other parts of the Mabinogion tales were analysed very interestingly and provocatively by the late W. J. Gruffydd; and his method of procedure consisted to a large extent of comparisons with material in Irish literature and folklore. The same comparative vein has more recently been very successfully exploited by Dr. Proinsias Mac Cana in a book both brilliant and judicious,[1] and there can be no doubt that the clue to an important element in early Welsh tradition is to be found along these lines. I believe, however, that comparisons within the rather closed circle of the Celtic literatures do not necessarily exhaust all the possibilities of fruitful study, and that in addition to the method of research just mentioned, universally accepted as it is, there is another side to the problem; one which has on the whole received very little attention indeed from writers on early Welsh literature. I propose to explore this approach in these Gregynog Lectures, chiefly but not solely with reference to the Mabinogion. I shall devote the first two lectures to a discussion of the study of the international popular tale as it is interpreted by folklorists nowadays, since this is a subject which seems to have attracted rather little notice in Wales in the last generation, at any rate in print; and in the last two lectures I shall consider the application of this to the traditions preserved in early Welsh literature.

In the first place, what is meant by the term 'the popular tale'? We are familiar with the expression 'the folk-tale', which was invented because the existence of stories of this kind was first consciously recognized by educated and sophisticated people among the rural peasantry of Europe, and they assumed that they belonged essentially, and had always so belonged, to what they called the 'folk'. This usage can be traced back to the eighteenth century, and the concept at least to the seventeenth, and these things are aspects of that romantic attitude to the peasant which has so often made its appearance among the upper and middle classes ever since the Renaissance. The idea, and particularly the use of the word 'folk' in these connexions, has had unfortunate results, expressions of which are still with us in spite of the researches, extending over more than a century, of the people we call 'folklorists'. I say 'unfortunate' because it has caused the true character of the popular tale to become obscured in the minds of many people. Those who are not very conversant with this form of literature and its history often tend to regard it as something necessarily very childish, very inartistic and crude, and as the almost exclusive property of mentally backward, ignorant, and boorish yokels, apart from the very occasional patronizing use of folktale plots by the literary classes when it happens to suit them.[2]

The fact is, however, that the rigid distinction drawn in modern times between the popular literature of the 'folk' and the popular literature of other classes was to some degree unreal and without meaning before the close of the Middle Ages. The spread of general literacy among the upper and middle classes that came with the Renaissance, and the increasing sophistication which it involved, was the beginning of a split between them and the rural lower classes which has persisted in its effects ever since. Among its first manifestations was the extra-ordinary idealization of the life of the shepherd and shepherdess so characteristic of the sixteenth and seven-teenth centuries—another, as I have already hinted, was the appearance in the seventeenth century of the first literary collections of popular tales which are self-consciously treated as imitated from the 'Folk'. With the Industrial Revolution the divergence was vastly in-creased, and society was further divided into the urban and the rural. In the end the result in modern times has been that the educated city dweller often has about as much comprehension of the mind of the so-called 'yokel' as if the latter were a native of Patagonia; hence some curious theories still popularly current among some anthropologists and students of folklore who derive their inspiration from Frazer's *Golden Bough*. In fact in highly industrialized countries like England the oral folktale is now all but extinct, and has been so for a long time. The only kind which really survives to any extent is the humorous tale; and the only class of truly *oral* tale, handed on by word of mouth and very seldom finding its way into print, now still remaining in sophisticated urban society is what is politely called 'the smoking room story'. But before the Renaissance the stories genuinely popular and current among the upper classes had a great deal more in common with those popular with the unlettered peasantry, and their plots were very often the same. The same tales would entertain princes and paupers, the Knight and the Miller, as may be seen from a glance at the Canterbury Tales. Hence there was a constant give and take between the two, a constant process whereby literary men adopted stories from folk sources and folktale tellers made use of material which they acquired in various ways from literary sources. Endless examples could be quoted where a given tale turns up again and again both in literature and in oral folklore, and it is really not possible to say to which it properly belongs, or indeed what this distinction means. I shall quote some instances a little later in this lecture. For all these reasons I prefer to use the term 'popular tale', not 'folktale', because I shall be discussing stories which were popular at one time with all classes and not merely with the 'folk'. When I do say 'folktale' I shall mean not a *class* of story but a story in a particular context, current among and collected from the 'folk'.

In treating the popular tale as a single entity I am, of course, referring in the first place to the essential *plots*. The *style* of the telling is generally different and may be very different. Up to a point, each has its own conventions of style. Thus in a folk context the characters are practically universally anonymous—'the young man', 'the princess', 'the king', and so on, or at most they have simple names like 'Jack' or 'Hans'. The places mentioned are anonymous equally—'the land beyond the North Wind', 'the land of the giants', 'the town', and such like. The exception is where a tale becomes attached to some known figure of popular renown, such as King Arthur or Robin Hood, whether genuinely historical or merely legendary. In a literary context these features always tend to be named, and hence Chaucer tells a well-known popular tale about 'Grisilde' and makes the scene of it 'Saluzzo' in Piedmont, where a folktale teller would have made her 'the girl' or 'the king's wife', and if he named the country at all it would be 'the Land of the Blue Mountains' or some such place. Or again, in folk contexts, though kings and queens are favourite characters, the life they lead is that of a prosperous farmer, so that the king answers his own front door bell and the queen is familiar with the herds of pigs; whereas in the literary version court life may be very much better understood and the whole treatment may be courtly.

These differences, however, are really superficial. All versions of popular tales, whether literary or folk, have certain features in common in addition to the fundamental identity of plot, and these features contrast very clearly with the characteristics of the artistic tale invented by the literary artist. They are mostly dictated by the fact that the popular tale in its origins and in much of its transmission is essentially oral and consequently recited to a popular audience. Thus there is no real characterization, which would take too long and would be irrelevant to the purpose of the narrative, besides being too subtle for many audiences; hence we have stock characters such as the stupid man, the cunning man, the wicked witch, the strong hero, and the rest. Again, the popular tale must not be too long to try the patience of the audience and tax the reciter's memory too far, nor should it be too sophisticated or otherwise too specialized to meet with general appreciation and understanding. It must be interesting and must have a 'point' which can be successfully put across; otherwise no one would care to remember and tell it or listen to it. It never aims at originality, and the reciter never mentions himself (except sometimes in certain opening and closing formulas), and never obtrudes his personality in any way, least of all in the folktale.³ In short, the popular tale is a kind of general common denominator of narrative—I do not say 'lowest common denominator'—whose nature has been dictated by its essentially oral and universal character, but which was formerly as much at home in the baronial hall as in the cottage of the serf.

This does not mean—and this is something that I want to stress very strongly at the outset—that stories recited orally by folktale tellers are necessarily crude and inartistic and told in a clumsy, stumbling, pedestrian manner. The reverse is very much the case. Any decent folktale teller is an artist, and some of the finest stories ever told have been collected from their oral recitation. This is something which the ordinary cloistered scholar finds it very difficult to believe and even to understand, because he often knows absolutely nothing at first hand about the living folktale. It is very strange that so many scholars weave theories about the history of oral tales and early literature when they have no practical experience whatever of the folktale as it really is; and there is no excuse for this state of affairs in these islands, where a splendid tradition of folktale telling is still alive in the west of Ireland and the Highlands, available for study by anyone who takes the trouble to learn the languages. What I have just said about the artistic skill of folktale reciters is particularly applicable to the Gaelic shanachies of Scotland and Ireland, who are masters in the art of handling complicated plot and incident and absolute masters of oral prose style. Many examples could be quoted, but to pick one at random I should like to refer to the Scottish Gaelic tale *An Crochaire Lom-Rusgach* in Macdougall's *Folk and Hero Tales*;[4] a story of over 12,000 words told by an Argyllshire roadmender, and one of the best folk-tales for plot, construction, and style that I have ever met —the performance of a fine artist. And this is nothing very exceptional.

Thus far, then, for the moment an explanation of what I mean by 'the popular tale'. But what about the adjective 'international'? This can perhaps best be made clear by an example. When I first went down to West Kerry to learn Irish, almost thirty years ago, I used to practise it by writing down in phonetic script the stories told me daily by that queen of folktale tellers, Peig Sayers. One tale which she told me,[5] and which she declared was a true one, was in summary as follows: There was a Jew who married a Christian woman, and he himself turned Christian, as he thought it would prosper his business. He grew rich, and at last decided he was tired of being a Christian and would return to his people. He invited the priest to dinner on a Friday, and set a roast turkey before him. The priest said, 'Aren't you a Christian, and don't you know we don't eat meat on Fridays?' 'Och, take it easy, we'll soon put that to rights', said the Jew, and he fetched a bowl of water and began to sprinkle the turkey, saying, 'Become fish!' 'Are you out of your senses?' asked the priest. 'Why,' said the Jew, 'isn't that how you made me a Christian? You sprinkled me with water and said "Become Catholic!", but you could no more make a Christian of me that way than I can make a fish of the turkey.' The priest left in a rage, and the Jew became a Hebrew again.

Now, when I got back to London on this occasion it happened that I was dining with my old friend Ifor Evans, late Principal of this College. Another guest was a member of the Roumanian Embassy, who astonished me by repeating this selfsame story and declaring it had actually occurred in Roumania. A few days later I spoke of this to my neighbour at High Table at my college, G. C. Coulton, the medieval historian. 'Oh,' said Coulton, 'that's an old tale', and he referred me to an eighteenth-century French source where it is related of a Turk in Italy.[6] Some years afterwards I happened upon exactly the same thing told in Australia about a missionary and an Australian aborigine who wanted to eat meat on Good Friday.[7] Finally, when I was studying Yiddish as a language and a source for folklore some years later I discovered a Yiddish version about a Jew and a priest in a collection of Jewish tales from Poland,[8] very remarkably close to the Irish one I heard on the Blasket Island. I have little doubt that the tale is in fact of Jewish origin.[9]

I have deliberately chosen a rather ludicrous example to illustrate the extraordinary ubiquity of the popular tale. The fact is that what is quite obviously one single tale with unquestionably one single origin may often be found, not simply widespread, but in almost any part of the habitable earth, and sometimes occurring in written literature from the oldest literary works of man down to the present day. These popular tales are not merely ubiquitous, they are indestructible and immortal; again and again they turn up, until it becomes really quite monotonous. And I am not referring merely to simple anecdotes with only one episode, like that I have just told, but also to very long tales with involved and subdivided plots. I propose now to summarize a number of instances of this in detail, to make quite clear both the international character of the international popular tale and its popularity; and also the way in which it appears continually and freely in literary sources as well as in oral folklore.

Let me begin with one of the most popular of all as well as one of the most highly complicated for its wealth of episodes both major and minor—the story known to folklorists as The Magic Flight.[10] The skeleton summary of this international tale given in Aarne and Thompson's great classification[11] is as follows:

(1) *Hero comes into Ogre's power.* A boy promises himself to an ogre in settlement of a gambling debt. [Or], he sees girls (transformed swans) bathing in a lake and steals the swan coat of one of them; she agrees to marry him and takes him home to her father's house. [Or], the hero pursues a bird to the Ogre's house.

(2) *The Ogre's tasks.* The Ogre forbids the hero to enter one certain chamber. [Or], the Ogre assigns the hero impossible tasks (planting a vineyard, cleaning a stable, washing black yarn white, cutting down a forest, catching a magic horse, sorting grains, &c.), which are performed with the magic help of the Ogre's daughter. He must choose his wife from her sisters who look magically alike; by means of a missing finger (lost in the process of killing and resuscitating her) the hero chooses correctly.

(3) *The Flight.* In preparation for the flight they leave behind them magic speaking objects. In their flight they transform themselves into various persons and things to deceive the Ogre, for instance, rose and thornbush,

church and priest, &c. [and/] or they throw behind them magic objects (comb, stone, flint) which become ob-stacles (forest, mountain, fire) in the path of the pursuer. [Or] they escape over a magic bridge which folds up behind them. [The tale may end at this point, but gener-ally it continues with]

(4) *The Forgotten Fiancée.* The hero forgets his bride when, against her warning, he kisses his mother (or his dog) or tastes food on his visit home.

(5) *Waking from Magic Forgetfulness.* The bride buys a place for three nights in the bridal bed from her husband's new bride; not till the third night does he wake. [Or], the girl attracts attention to herself by magically placing three lovers in embarrassing positions; [or] by magically stopping the wedding carriage, [or] by a conversation between herself and objects or animals, [or] by the con-versation of two magic birds displayed at the wedding, [or] by transformations or otherwise.

(6) *The Old Bride Chosen.* Between the new and the old bride the choice is made according to the adage about the old key that has been found again.

Such is the summary. The various alternatives mean that in any one version one (or occasionally more) of the alternatives will be found but not the others; nevertheless, it is unquestionably the same tale in all cases. This is one of the longest and most complicated of all international tales, as well as one of the finest. Versions have been collected in modern times from oral recitation all over Europe, as well as in Siberia, Turkey, North America, and even Samoa. It is popular in Ireland and Scotland. I have collected two myself in Scottish Gaelic in the Hebrides, and I will summarize one of these, from Barra, running to nearly 5,000 words,[12] as an example of the actual tale in practice as distinct from the composite skeleton:

The hero plays cards with a strange horseman, and having lost the third game is put under *geasa* or magical obligations to discover where the horseman lives before a year is out. His uncle tells him that the stranger's three daughters come in the form of swans to a certain lake once a year to bathe, and advises him to steal one of their swan dresses when they have put them off, and extract a promise to tell him how to find the stranger as the price of returning the dress. He does this, and the girl, having re-ceived back her swan dress, flies with him to her father's house. Once he is there, the father sets him a series of im-possible tasks—to clean out a filthy cow-shed, to thatch it with birds' feathers, and to catch three wild fillies on the mountain. These tasks are accomplished by the magic help of the daughter. (The girl loses a toe in the process, and the recognition motif which appears later should have followed from this, but this story teller has trans-posed it to a later stage.) The couple then flee on a horse, pursued by the girl's father. She tells the hero to throw behind them what he finds in the left ear of the horse (presumably a splinter of wood). He does so, and it grows into a forest through which the father is unable to make his way till he returns home and fetches two axes. He then catches up with the couple again; and on the girl's advice the hero throws behind them what he finds in the right ear of the horse (presumably a drop of sweat), and it becomes a lake. The father cannot cross it, and must return home for two balers to bale it out, but before he has finished baling the couple have finally escaped and got safely to the hero's home. The girl now says she will not go home with him for the present; that he is to get things ready for her, but to be careful to kiss no one, for if he does he will forget her. But his father's dog licks his face, and at once he forgets about the girl. A great feast is made,[13] and the girl comes to it with a magic golden cock and silver hen, and three steel bands round her chest. She throws a grain to the hen and the cock snatches it, and the hen says, 'You would not have done that if you remembered how I cleaned out the cow-shed for you'; and one of the steel bands snaps. This is repeated, with reference to thatching the cow-shed and again with reference to catching the wild fillies; and when the hen speaks of thatching the cow-shed the girl shows the company that she has lost a toe, and at each recital one of the steel bands snaps. At last the hero remembers the girl, and they are married.

This is an example of the story of The Magic Flight collected on the western edge of Europe in Scottish Gaelic in 1952. Now, as an example of a literary version, at least nine centuries older, I will describe very briefly the tale of Sringabhuja[14] in the *Kathasaritsagara* or 'Ocean of the Streams of Story', a great collection of Sanskrit popular tales compiled by Somadeva in the eleventh century. The hero shoots at and wounds a demon in the form of a crane, and follows him to his castle. There, he is set difficult tasks by the demon and performs them with the help of his daughter. He successfully recognizes her among her seemingly identical sisters because she has piled her necklace on top of her head whereas the others have theirs round their necks. He has to sow a hundred three-bushel measures of seed and gather every single seed in again; the daughter does this for him, using her magic to make a troop of ants bring in the seeds. The couple are to be married, and the demon sends the hero to his brother to invite him to the wedding—really intending that he shall kill the hero. However, he escapes from the brother, who pursues him, by throwing behind him earth, water, thorns, and fire; the first three become respectively a mountain, a river, and a forest, which delay the pursuer, and the fire stops him. The hero and the girl then ride away on a horse with the demon father in pursuit, but the girl twice makes the hero and the horse invisible and herself puts her father off the scent by changing into a woodcutter and a letter carrier and giving false information, and the couple escape to the hero's home. The tale ends here, and there is no sequel about forgetting and recognition; but no one could doubt that this ancient Indian story is essentially identical with the modern Scottish one as well as with the hundreds of other versions which have been collected and which are in various respects even closer to the Sanskrit.

Another instance of the same striking character is the Greek myth of Perseus and Andromeda. You will remember that Andromeda is exposed as a sacrifice to a sea-monster and rescued by Perseus who kills it. This forms the central episode in a popular tale called The Dragon Slayer[15] of which well over one thousand oral folk versions have been recorded, the vast majority from Europe, though it is also known in Asia (including Japan and Malaya), in North and Central Africa, in North America, the Caribbean, and Brazil. It is familiar in Irish and Scottish Gaelic; I have collected a Gaelic version myself in Nova Scotia.[16] There are a number of distinct redactions or editions, some of which are found in some areas and others in others. The probability is that it is a very old story indeed, which has been disseminated, and specialized in various separate ways in various areas, for a great many centuries. The Greek myth is simply an early instance taken from some version of the popular tale current in ancient Greece.

A story closely connected with The Dragon Slayer, and into which the latter is indeed often inserted, is the one known as The Two Brothers.[17] There is a childless couple, and one day the man catches a magic fish, which tells him to cut it up and give parts to eat to his wife, his dog, and his mare. They each have twins as a result, and in due course the boys grow up and each has his own dog and horse. The elder twin goes travelling with his two animals, and leaves behind an object which will change its appearance if he gets into danger—it is commonly a tree which will wither—the motif called a 'life token'. He goes to a distant land and is married to a princess. Later he comes to the house of a witch, who pretends to be scared of his dog and asks him to tie it up, and gives him one of her hairs to use for the purpose. When this is done she attacks the youth, who calls on his dog for help, but the hair becomes a chain and the dog cannot move; and the witch turns the youth to a stone. At home, the younger twin brother sees from the changed appearance of his life token that his brother is in deadly danger. He goes to seek him, and comes by chance to the very city where his brother is now king; everyone takes him for his elder brother, including his wife, and he is obliged to fall in with this and consequently to sleep with his brother's wife. However, he lays a sword between them in bed as a chastity token, and keeps it there. He then traces his brother to the witch's house. When she gives him a hair to tie up his dog he only pretends to do so, and when she attacks him the dog comes to his aid. They overcome her and she is forced to reveal where the brother is. With her magic wand he disenchants the brother, and then they kill the witch.

The distribution of this enormously popular tale is similar to that of The Dragon Slayer; it is especially a favourite in Europe. Nearly 800 folk versions of it have been collected—including sixty-five German, sixty-six Danish, twenty-eight Czech, twenty-seven Italian, and so on, and it is well known in Irish and particularly Scottish Gaelic. The essential and central theme is that the older of two brothers goes travelling and is killed by the guile of a woman, and the younger knows by a token that he is dead, searches for his body, and resuscitates him by magic; and this fundamental kernel of the story was known already as early as about 1250 B.C. in Egypt in the tale of Anupu and Bitiu which exists in a papyrus of that date.[18] Most folklorists agree that this is in fact an exceedingly ancient version of the core of the tale of The Two Brothers, which is thus one of the oldest known international popular tales in the world. This is another very fine example of the fact that a modern folktale widely popular in various parts of the world may have behind it an enormously long history; I stress this now because I should like you to remember it when I come to deal with Welsh sources.

The story best known in these islands as King John and the Abbot of Canterbury[19] may be mentioned as a further instance with a considerable history, though nothing like so long. The king is angry with his minister and threatens to put him to death unless he can answer certain riddling questions; these vary considerably, but favourite ones are 'How long would it take me to go round the world?', 'How much am I worth?', and 'What am I thinking?' The minister is in despair, but his brother the shepherd or miller undertakes to disguise himself as the minister and answer the questions. He does this successfully; the solutions of the riddles just mentioned are, 'If you rose with the sun and travelled with it, it would take you 24 hours to go round the earth'; 'You are worth 29 pence, because Christ was sold for 30 pence and you are not quite so worthy as him'; and 'You think I am your minister but I am not, I am his brother the shepherd'. The king is so amused and pleased by these cunning answers that he forgives the minister and all ends happily.

The story has been the subject of a study by Walter Anderson, who lists nearly 600 known versions in eighteen different identifiable 'editions' or redactions. The oldest instance is a Coptic version from Egypt noted by the Arabian writer Ibn ʿAbd el-Hakem about A.D. 850. As a folktale it has been recorded all over Europe (Ireland and Scotland included) and in parts of Asia, including Siberia, India, and Ceylon. The especially interesting feature of this story, however, apart from its appearance in the ninth century in Egypt, is the fact that more than a quarter of the 600-odd versions are not modern oral folktales but early, medieval, and early modern written literary ones, among which may be mentioned a thirteenth-century French one by Étienne de

Bourbon and the well-known English ballad of King John and the Abbot of Canterbury which goes back to the sixteenth century. I would emphasize this high proportion of literary treatments of an international pop- ular tale, as it illustrates very clearly the fact that such stories continually appear in literary sources all through history and are by no means simply the property, exclu- sive or otherwise, of 'plowmen, goose-girls, blacksmiths, midwives, or yokels', to quote a recent writer. It is im- portant to bear this in mind when the Welsh material is discussed presently. Anderson in his study has made it probable that the story is of Jewish origin, dating from perhaps the seventh century; and he believes it was brought to Europe by the Crusaders, though this is by no means certain.

A tale of a very different type, but traceable to almost exactly the same period as the Coptic story of The King and his Vizir, is our old friend Cinderella.[20] This is a story of enormous popularity. Over 700 oral versions have been collected in Europe alone, Irish and Scottish Gaelic ones among them, and it is found also in Asia (including China and Japan), North Africa, and North and South America (including American Indian). The oldest known instance is a Chinese story of the ninth century A.D., but in Europe it does not turn up until the seventeenth-century Italian *Pentamerone* of Basile and the French *Contes de Ma Mère l'Oye* or 'Tales of Mother Goose' of Charles Perrault. It may perhaps surprise some of us to hear that Cinderella is first recorded in China, and over 1,000 years ago, but this is simply a further example of the fantastic history of the international popular tale.

These two examples which can be traced back to the ninth century A.D. are, however, mere infants by comparison with another favourite, The Master Thief,[21] for the oldest version of this is told in the fifth century B.C. by Herodotus[22] in his tale of Rhampsinitus, and is believed to have been used even earlier by Eugammon of Cyrene. A thief is caught robbing a king's treasury, in a trap from which it is impossible to free him, so that he must inevitably be discovered. To prevent recognition and the consequent tracing of his accomplices he gets his brother, who is with him, to cut off his head and escape with it. But the king is determined to discover the robbers, and he has the headless body paraded in the streets, hoping that the relatives will be seen weeping; and later the brother steals the body from the guards by making them drunk, or by some other ruse. Lastly the king advertises that his daughter is to sleep with all comers on condition they tell her what was the most dangerous feat they ever did. The brother takes advantage of this, and tells her his story, and she marks his forehead with a black mark— in secret, as she thinks. But the thief has noticed it, and he himself later secretly marks all the king's courtiers, and even the king himself, with the same mark, so that once again no one knows who it was. The last motif is somewhat different in Herodotus.

This is generally believed to have been of Egyptian origin—and it is notable that once again Egypt plays an important early part in the history of an international popular tale. The story reached India early enough to be incorporated into the legend of Buddha, as appears from a third-century Chinese translation and from the Tibetan *Kanjur* of the ninth to thirteenth centuries; and there is a rather poor version in the eleventh-century Sanskrit *Katha-saritsagara*.[23] In Europe it is found already in the late twelfth-century Latin *Dolopathos* of Johannes de Alta Silva, and rather more developed in the early thirteenth-century French adaptation of this by the troubadour Herbert; and also in the closely related collection of tales popularly known as *The Seven Sages of Rome*, the oldest copy of which is a French version of about 1155. In this way it reached Wales, in time to appear in the Red Book of Hergest in the Welsh rendering of that collection, the *Chwedleu Seith Doethon Rufein*, edited by Professor Henry Lewis. This is a fine example of an international popular tale in medieval Wales, and one which got there for certain by means of a chain of literary translations. But quite apart from the great popularity in European litera-ture which the story acquired by being included in the widely disseminated *Seven Sages of Rome*, the Rhamp-sinitus story is scattered all over the Old World as a folktale, from Iceland, Ireland, and Scotland in the north-west to the Philippines in the south-east.

The Two Travellers is a good example of an old and very widespread tale found both in literary sources and oral folklore.[24] Two travelling men have a dispute whether truth or falsehood is best. The man who sup-ports truth loses the argument and is blinded (or the motif of the blinding may arise in other ways). He wan-ders around and spends the night under a tree, where he overhears demons or magic cats or other animals talking, and learns from this how to restore his own sight, how to cure a sick princess or king, where a treasure is buried, and other valuable information. He accordingly regains his sight, cures the sick person, digs up the treasure, and so on. When the dishonest companion hears of this he imitates the other by hiding in the same place to listen to the supernatural creatures, but is torn to pieces by them.

The tale can be traced back to early India, and some think it as old there as the fourth century; it is found first in a Chinese text of the year 710 translated from Indian sources, and also in the ninth- to thirteenth-century Tibetan *Kanjur*, likewise a translation from Sanskrit material, of a much earlier date. It is in the Sanskrit *Panchatantra*, which cannot be later than the sixth century A.D.; in a collection of Hebrew tales not later than the tenth century and perhaps much earlier;[25] in the eleventh-century Sanskrit *Kathasaritsagara*;[26] and also in the Persian *Haft Paikar* of Nisami, composed in 1197; the Hebrew *Midrash Haggadol*, a commentary on the Pentateuch not later than the fourteenth century;[27] and in the Arabian Nights. There is no need to detail the later literary tellings of it in Europe, where it tended to be used as a moral exemplum. As an oral folktale it is popular throughout almost the whole of Europe and Asia, and has been recorded in North and Central Africa and in North America. It seems certain that The Two Travellers is of Asiatic origin, very likely Indian.

My last example is the story known as 'What should I have Said?'[28] A stupid boy is given a message to repeat, but gets it muddled and repeats the wrong words, resulting in a series of confusions and ending in disaster. A good version of this was recorded in Essex at the beginning of last century.[29] The boy's mother sends him out to buy a sheep's head and pluck, but he forgets the correct message, and goes his way reciting aloud, 'Liver and lights and gall and all'. He comes upon a man who is ill and vomiting, and passes by, saying, 'Liver and lights and gall and all'. The man is angry, and beats him, and tells him he should say 'Pray God send no more up'; so the boy goes his way, chanting 'Pray God send no more up'—and meets a farmer sowing wheat. The farmer beats the boy and tells him he should say 'Pray God send plenty more'. This he does as he passes by a funeral cortège, with the usual result; and is told to say 'Pray God send the soul to Heaven'. Next he meets some people about to hang a couple of dogs, which was the standard way of killing dogs in the days before gas; and he repeats 'Pray God send the soul to Heaven'. Once again he is beaten, and told to say 'A dog and a bitch going to be hanged'. The next thing he meets is a wedding party, and on his reciting these words he is again beaten, and told to say 'I wish you much joy'. This he says on finding two men who have fallen into a ditch, and one has just climbed out; and he is told to say, 'One is out, I wish the other was'. So he duly repeats this when he meets a one-eyed man, who orders him to say 'The one side gives good light, I wish the other did'. Finally he arrives at a house on fire, and when he chants these words he is arrested, charged with arson, and hanged.

Compare this with the modern Chinese folktale.[30] A fool is swimming, and a beggar steals his clothes. A funeral goes by, and the fool takes the pall to cover himself, but the mourners chase and beat him. When he gets home his wife says he should have said 'My sympathy'. Next day he sees a wedding party, and says 'My sympathy', and is again beaten—he should have said 'Congratulations'. Then he finds a house on fire, and expresses his congratulations, and is told he should have helped to put it out. The story ends with his getting killed by two bulls which are fighting and which he tries to separate. As in this Chinese version, the tale may include 'What should I have done?' as well as 'What should I have said?', or the latter may often appear by itself. In addition to China and Japan, it is found in modern folklore pretty well throughout Europe and in other parts of Asia, and also in the United States. The oldest known version is in the Chinese translation of the Buddhist *Tripitaka*, fifth century A.D., and the tale is believed to be of Buddhist origin.

I have summarized and dealt with the history of these stories in some detail because it illustrates so well what is meant by the 'international popular tale'. It shows its ubiquity and indestructibility; the tales are found in enormous numbers of versions throughout the Old World from Ireland to Japan, and frequently in the New World. Moreover, quite often they can be traced back to ancient times—in one case to the thirteenth century B.C.; and it is remarkable how often India, and only less frequently Egypt and Greece, figure in the early history of a tale. Some stories have had a considerable vogue in literature, such as The Two Travellers, and others seem to have had their life chiefly as oral popular tales; but practically always there is this striking fact that they continually alternate between popularity in literature and popularity in folklore. I should like to elaborate this point a little further, so that there can be no possible doubt about it when the Welsh examples are discussed.

First, a couple of instances of stories current especially orally but having literary adaptations of unusual interest.

There is the tale of the stupid ogre, a dangerous threat to the hero, who asks him what his name is. 'Myself', says the hero. Later he attacks the ogre, who screams for help. The neighbouring ogres come running to the house and shout, 'Who is hurting you?' 'Myself', shrieks the ogre from inside. 'Oh well,' say the others, 'if you are such a fool as to hurt yourself we can't help you', and they go away.[31] This story has immense popularity as a folktale in large parts of Asia and all through Europe; including England, Ireland, and Scotland. In Scotland it is told about the wild glen-dwelling demon called *ùruisg*, and how the clever woman got rid of one which bothered her, by scalding its bare legs with boiling water or porridge and employing the 'Myself' ruse.[32] The name given is generally 'Myself', but in some places 'Nobody' is preferred—so, 'Nobody is hurting me'. In literature the tale is found in the twelfth-century Latin *Dolopathos* referred to above, and in the Arabian Nights, but, of course, the most famous instance is the episode with Polyphemus in the Odyssey. There is very little doubt that this was an extremely ancient popular jest which was known at least as early as the eighth century B.C. and probably much earlier, and was used by Homer or his predecessors in the literary epic of Odysseus. The reverse, that its wide distribution as a folktale derives from the Odyssey, has been shown to be very much less likely.

Then, I would refer to a literary treatment of the great complex of stories called The Grateful Dead Man,[33] which are immensely widespread as oral tales. I have myself collected a Scottish Gaelic version in Nova Scotia.[34] The oldest known example of this is the story of Tobias and the Angel in the Apocryphal Book of

Tobit. Baldly, the essentials are that by the supernatural aid of a grateful dead man the hero wins a bride who is in alliance with a demon and therefore has to be disenchanted, which is done by cutting her in half and driving out the snakes inside her, and then fitting her together again. This story was adopted into the chivalrous romantic literature of medieval France,[35] and certain alterations were made so that it would suit that very specialized social and intellectual setting. The grateful dead man gives the hero a horse and weapons and helps him win a bride in a tournament; she is to be cut in half and divided as the winnings, but the dead man lets the hero keep her unhurt. This artificial romantic treatment is found in Europe from the thirteenth century, in French, Italian, German, Swedish, and Middle English[36] romances, and in Straparola's sixteenth-century collection of Italian tales.[37] A further modification of the medieval period is that the role of the grateful dead man is played by a saint, and the whole thing becomes part of the saint's legend. This literary treatment has scarcely found its way back into folklore at all, but this is no doubt because the folktale tellers would recognize it as a, to them, inferior version of the standard tale which they preferred. The point at the moment is that in spite of the really rather superficial literary alterations the story is unquestionably the same, and it is a good example of the interchange between folklore and literature.

The reverse interchange, the spread in oral folklore of tales which are of literary origin or have certainly their chief life in literature, or have been disseminated in the first place from written or printed sources, may also easily be demonstrated. A rather remarkable instance is quoted concerning a historical incident of the Sung dynasty in China which became the subject of literary novels and plays, but eventually developed in modern times into a regular popular oral folktale of the 'per-secuted wife' type.[38] A story which seems to have had a life primarily in literature but is also quite well known in folklore in certain specific forms is the one called The Ring of Polycrates.[39] The essential feature is that a ring is lost, or deliberately thrown away, in water, and it is expected that it will never be found again; but it had been swallowed by a fish, which is caught, and the ring is discovered. The classic instance is, of course, the story of Polycrates in Herodotus.[40] Polycrates is exceed-ingly rich and powerful, and the king of Egypt warns him to throw away his most precious possession as a means of placating the jealousy of the gods. Polycrates throws a ring in the sea, but it is swallowed by a fish which is caught and presented to Polycrates. The ring is discovered, and when the king of Egypt hears of this he knows that Polycrates is doomed.

The motif has had great popularity in literature, and has been used in a variety of different applications, none of them the same as Herodotus's. For one thing, it was adopted in medieval hagiography as follows: a holy man is overcome with a sense of sin for some deed, and throws a ring or key into the water, swearing he will never cease his penance till it is found, or other similar oath. It is later discovered in a fish. The story is told in this form of St. Egwin of Worcester, St. Arnould of Metz, St. Mauri-lius of Angers, St. Attilanus of Zamora, St. Gerbold of Bayeux, St. Ambrose of Cahors, and particularly of St. Gregory the Great, in which case it was combined

with the Oedipus tale. The legend of Gregory goes back
to a ninth-century Coptic Christian source which was
adopted in Western Europe and applied to St. Gregory
in the eleventh century. The Gregory story has found its
way into folklore.[41] A rather different religious application is seen in a sixteenth- or seventeenth-century Spanish
legend of St. Antony. A man loses a ring in the sea; he
has masses said in honour of St. Antony, and the ring is
found in a fish. One may compare the tale in the *Life of
St. Cadog*[42] about how Cadog lost his book at sea but a
fisherman brought him a fish with the book inside it.
Still another application of the basic tale to the legend of
a saint is found in the story associated with St. Bridget.[43]
In Cogitosus's Latin *Life of St. Bridget*, of the middle of
the seventh century, a certain Irish nobleman wishes to
get a woman as his mistress; he entrusts a brooch to her,
but then abstracts it and throws it in the sea, so that he
can enslave her when she fails to produce it. The woman
appeals to St. Bridget, and the brooch is duly found in
the usual way. The Irish *Lives* of St. Bridget, which may
belong to the ninth century, have the story with the
slight change that it is a jealous wife who tries to get her
husband's maid into trouble by throwing the ring in the
sea; but a Portuguese tale of manuscript origin has the
story exactly as in Cogitosus, from whom it must ultimately derive.[44] A modern Spanish and Portuguese folktale tells how a girl disguised as a man is falsely accused
of attempted rape by a queen by the Potiphar's Wife ruse:
the enraged queen sets her tasks, including finding a ring
lost at sea, but the girl invokes St. Peter and a fish is caught
with the ring in it. The German legend of St. Verena of
Zurzach, who was a maid in a house where a valuable

ring was lost, and, being ordered to fish in the Rhine, caught a salmon with the ring in it, may perhaps come from Cogitosus; but a more interesting relative is found in the eighth- or ninth-century Irish *Táin Bó Fraích* and the twelfth-century Scottish *Life of St. Kentigern*.[45] Here the ring is given by a woman to a man as a love token, and this is discovered by the woman's relatives, who suspect her of sexual misconduct, secretly throw the ring in the water, and threaten her with death if she cannot produce it. The ring is, however, found in the standard way; in the Scottish version owing to the intervention of St. Kentigern. This particular application of The Ring of Polycrates seems to be of Irish origin, probably a modi-fication of the story as seen in the *Life of St. Bridget*.

Other treatments have nothing to do with saints. The fourth- to eighth-century Sanskrit play *Sakuntala* has a rajah give Sakuntala a ring so that he can recognize her when they meet again; she loses it, he does not recognize her, and rebuffs her, but it is found in a fish and all is well. The motif is further applied to love and sex in a number of other tales. In a modern Kashmir folktale a girl loses a ring in water, a fish is served at the palace, the ring is found in it, and the king proclaims that whoever has lost it is to come to him. The girl comes, and he falls in love with her. In the English ballad of 'The Cruel Knight upon the Road', and in the story of Miss Elton of Stratford, a gentleman discovers that a certain low-born girl is fated to be his wife. He twice tries to have her killed, and on failing he throws the ring in the sea and swears she shall never be his wife till she brings him the ring. The result is as usual. This has been a favourite subject of story in chapbooks, ballads, and folktales in

Britain, and is found also as a ballad in France and as a folktale in Portugal.

The legend of King Solomon's talismanic ring tells how he lost it in the sea, or it was thrown in the sea by a demon, and in consequence he lost all his power and wandered about in poverty; he either becomes a fisherman himself and catches a fish, or a fish is brought to him, but in either case it contains the ring and he recovers his kingdom. The story is a favourite with the Semitic peoples, being told in medieval Hebrew Rabbinical writings, in the Koran, the Arabian Nights, and Arabic folktales; there is a version in the Yiddish *Maasebuch* published at Basel in 1602.

In one form The Ring of Polycrates seems to have currency almost solely as a folktale, limited apparently almost exclusively to Scandinavia and north-west Germany.[46] A rich woman throws a ring in the water, saying, 'It is as likely that I shall ever be poor as it is that this ring will ever be found'; but it *is* found, in the regular way.[47] Finally, one or two isolated instances may be mentioned. One of the oldest known hails from China, in the Chinese translation of the Sanskrit *Tripitaka* of the third century B.C. A woman is fond of saying 'I lose nothing', and says it even when her son throws her ring in the sea. The standard sequel evokes the same triumphant statement. Again, the Caliph Haroun al Rashid has a valuable ruby which his brother covets, but he throws it in the Tigris, and after his brother dies it is found in a fish. The Provençal romance of Magalone tells how a bird snatches away a box containing three rings and drops it in the sea; the rings are found in a fish and brought to the hero's mother who recognizes them as belonging to her long-lost son, and believes him dead. Finally, a very simple treatment of The Ring of Poly-crates is found in the Newcastle tale of the man who loses a ring over a bridge and it is found years later in a fish.[48]

I have described the various versions of The Ring of Polycrates in some detail for two reasons. First, it shows the way in which a story whose life is primarily a literary one is capable of filtering down to the level of an ordinary oral folktale. Secondly, it is a splendid example of the protean changes, adaptations, and differentiations that a motif can undergo while still retaining its identity as one and the same tale. This could not happen to a long story of numerous motifs, like most of those I have summa-rized today, but a single, simple motif can be used in all sorts of ways, and The Ring of Polycrates is a particu-larly striking example. This will be seen to have con-siderable significance when I come to treat of the Welsh material.

Before leaving the subject of literary stories which get taken up in folklore I should like to mention the fact that the availability of cheap printed books has played a cer-tain part in the dissemination of tales among the folk in modern times, just as manuscript material did in an earlier period. The older generation of folklorists was very un-willing to admit this, because it seemed to detract from the value of the folktale as a very ancient thing and the exclusive or especial possession of the romanticized 'Folk', unable to read and therefore 'uncorrupted' by literature. Nevertheless, it certainly happens, and certainly did hap-pen with ancient and medieval written material. Two instances will show this, in respect of printed tales. The

Arabian Nights first became known in Europe at the beginning of the eighteenth century, and selections from it
were widely popular in the form of printed chapbooks. A
number of recorded folktales can be traced to this source.
The tale of the poor man who sees some robbers open the
door of a cave with the magic formula 'Open Sesame'
and follows their example, while his rich brother attempts
to imitate him and is killed, derives, of course, from Ali
Baba and the Forty Thieves in the Arabian Nights. It is
known as an oral tale in the folklore of most of Europe,
and in a fair number of instances the formula used contains a corruption of the word *sesame*; it follows that these
must come from printed chapbooks at very near removes,
since if the story had been a genuine oral folktale, *cognate*
as it were with the Arabic one, some phrase less foreign to
European botany would long ago have been substituted.

A further instance of what I mean is provided by an
Irish story I collected in West Kerry from Peig Sayers,[49]
who was my source for the story of the Christian Jew
already mentioned and many others. A certain man
left the church in disgust at the hypocrisy of the priest,
who was denouncing the sin of drunkenness though
himself a notorious drunkard. On the way home he
became thirsty, and a stranger who met him told him to
look over the wall, where he would find a stream from
which to drink. He looked, but the stream was flowing
through the carcass of a dead dog, and he refused to touch
it. But the stranger told him the water was pure and fit
to drink, and then explained the parable by saying that
the word of God preached by the priest was as pure as
this water though it came through a medium as corrupt
as the dead dog. Now this story is rare as a folktale, and

its source is the exempla or moral tales of the medieval preaching friars; in fact it comes from the *Gesta Roma-norum*, a collection of Latin romanticized exempla and other tales put together in England about 1300. The probability is that it gained currency as an oral tale in Ireland from the fact that an English printed version of stories from the *Gesta Romanorum* was used in the 'hedge schools' of eighteenth-century Ireland as a reading-book.

It is remarkable that some countries have a distinctly larger literary element in their oral folklore than others. India, with its very old and very extensive written com-pendiums of tales, which have continued to be read and popularized for many centuries, has in modern times an oral tradition which is full of literary influences. The same is true of modern Ireland and Gaelic Scotland; a notable part of many collections of oral tales gathered there consists of stories which are known to us in medie-val Irish literature, including some of the oldest and most familiar. Such are the tale of The Death of Cú Chulainn, that of Deirdre and the Sons of Uisneach, and that of Diarmaid and Gráinne, to mention only these. Diarmaid and Gráinne, The Death of Cú Chulainn, part of The Cattle Raid of Cooley, and the tale How Cú Chulainn Killed his Son Conlaoch, have all been collected recently from Gaelic oral recitation in the Hebrides by the School of Scottish Studies. O'Grady listed forty Fenian and other Irish romantic literary tales which were current popularly in manuscript in Munster in his time, and exactly 90 years later Delargy mentions seventeen of these which were still obtainable in Ireland from folk recita-tion, or had been in recent times.[50] Quite apart from the fact that there was no rigid separation into sophisticated and unsophisticated classes in medieval Ireland, the reason for this large literary element in Irish folklore is probably to be looked for in the wide dispersal among the folk of the sages, poets, and courtly entertainers of Ireland once the aristocratic order on which they depended had vanished away in the course of the seventeenth century.

Some of the stories which I have summarized consist of long and complicated recitals, with many episodes, such as The Magic Flight or The Two Brothers; others are much shorter, containing essentially only one or two simple themes, such as What Should I have Said? These have all been catalogued and indexed in the invaluable *Types of the Folktale*, by Antti Aarne and Stith Thompson, published at Helsinki in 1928, and commonly referred to as 'Aarne–Thompson' or simply 'AT.' It lists and summarizes over 700 stories, with a subsidiary roll of about 500 others, giving each a number and supplying the chief necessary bibliographical references enabling one to identify where the various printed versions, and studies on the individual tales, are to be found. 'Aarne–Thompson' classifies them into Animal Tales, Tales of Magic, Religious Tales, Novelle or Romantic Tales, Tales of the Stupid Ogre, Jokes and Anecdotes, and Formula Tales; and this classification has become accepted as the standard (though it is not completely satisfactory). 'Tales of Magic' are commonly called 'Wonder Tales', a term preferred by some folklorists; it means the class of story such as Cinderella or Snow-White in which the hero or heroine faces supernatural obstacles and overcomes them by supernatural means.

Apart from complete tales, popular narratives are made up of many separate episodes and numerous concepts, such as the help given the hero by grateful animals, the wicked stepmother who tries to get rid of her stepdaughter, the giant with one eye in the middle of his forehead, the idea that time in the Otherworld passes very quickly and unobserved by mortals who happen to be there, and so on. Many of them constitute an action, which makes them capable of existing as separate narratives in their own right, though not treated as such by Aarne–Thompson. These 'motifs' as they are called have been classified and numbered, with bibliographical references, by Stith Thompson in his great *Motif-Index of Folk Literature*, published at Helsinki in 1932–6, with a second edition published at Copenhagen in 1955–8. The index is known familiarly as 'Stith Thompson' or 'ST.' These two publications between them constitute indispensable working tools for the folklorist, and for those students of comparative literature who have realized —as many do not—that literature is something that can exist in speech as well as in writing. To these one must add the vast and immensely valuable five-volume commentary on Grimm's Fairy Tales by Johannes Bolte and Georg Polivka;[51] and, for anyone interested in Celtic literature, Tom Peete Cross's classification of early Irish narrative according to the Stith Thompson motif system, with some few excurses into Welsh.[52]

NOTES TO LECTURE I

[1] *Branwen Daughter of Llyr* (Cardiff, 1958).

[2] Compare the reference (*Folklore*, lxix, 2) by R. S. Loomis to 'plowmen, goose-girls, blacksmiths, midwives, or yokels of any kind'; and (ibid., p. 3) to 'the huts of plowmen or the haunts of peddlers'.

[3] Gruffydd is mistaken when he treats obtrusions of personality as a distinctive mark of oral recitation in general and of Irish folktales in particular. How he was able to say that 'A formula like "I know this tale to be true because I was present" is a regular feature' in Irish folktales it is difficult to understand (see Rh., pp. 2 f.). The absolute contrary is the usual case; when there is a closing formula the standard Irish one is 'That is my story, and if there is a lie in it, be it so; it is not I who composed or invented it'. This means, of course, not 'I have told what I myself witnessed' but 'I have told my tale as it was told to me'. Formulas which do imply, on the face of it, that the reciter was a witness (of the closing scene only) are comparatively rare and obviously humorous; moreover they do *not* say 'I know this tale to be true'.

[4] FHT.; text, pp. 112 ff., translation, pp. 76 ff.

[5] *Béaloideas*, viii, 52 f.

[6] Père Labat, *Voyages en Espagne et en Italie* (Paris, 1730), vi, 113.

[7] J. E. Lips, *The Savage Hits Back* (London, 1937), p. 44.

[8] Immanuel Olsvanger, *Rosinkess mit Mandlen* (Basel, 1931), no. 312.

[9] There is a very closely similar instance in Frey's collection of German humorous tales published in 1557 (see J. Bolte, *Jakob Frey's Gartengesellschaft*; Tübingen, 1896; p. 100).

[10] AT. 313. See the study by A. Aarne, FFC., no. 92; and by R. Christiansen, *Béaloideas*, i, 107; see also BP. ii, 516 ff.

[11] i.e. AT., see Abbreviations.

[12] Unpublished; in the collection of the School of Scottish Studies.

[13] The teller has forgotten the motif of the other bride and the wedding, and turns this into a feast.

[14] Tawney, i, 355 ff.

[15] AT. 300.

[16] *Scottish Gaelic Studies*, vi, 176 ff.

[17] AT. 303. See BP. i, 528, and the study on this tale by K. Ranke in FFC., no. 114.

[18] Masp., pp. 5 ff.

[19] AT. 922; see BP. iii, 214 ff., and the study by W. Anderson, *Kaiser und Abt*, in FFC., no. 42 (1923).

[20] AT. 510; see BP. i, 165 ff. and ii, 45 ff.; and M. R. Cox, *Cinderella* (London, 1893).

[21] AT. 950; see BP. iii, 395 ff.

[22] ii, 121.

[23] Tawney, op. cit. ii, 93.

[24] AT. 613; see BP. ii, 468 ff.; R. Christiansen, FFC., no. 24; A. Wesselski, *Märchen des Mittelalters* (Berlin, 1925), pp. 202 ff.; K. Krohn, FFC., no. 96, pp. 14 ff.

[25] See M. Gaster, *Folklore*, vii, 225 ff. and 231.

[26] Tawney, i, 263 f.

[27] See *Folklore*, i, 277; vii, 231.

[28] AT. 1696; see BP. iii, 145 ff.; M. Haavio, FFC., no. 88.

[29] *Folklore Record*, iii, 153.

[30] CFT., no. 110.

[31] AT. 1137; see BP. iii, 375 ff., and O. Hackman, *Die Polyphemsage in der Volksüberlieferung* (Helsinki, 1904).

[32] TGSI. xxv, 136; xxix, 27; *Irisleabhar Ceilteach*, I, iv, 98.

[33] AT. 507 A–C; see BP. iii, 83 ff. and 490 ff.; S. Liljeblad, *Die Tobias-geschichte* (Lund, 1927).

[34] *Scottish Gaelic Studies*, vi, 98 ff.

[35] See BP. iii, 507 ff. It is treated in AT. as a distinct tale, no. 508.

[36] Sir Amadas.

[37] *Piacevole Notti*, xi, 2.

[38] R. D. Jameson, *Three Lectures on Chinese Folklore* (Peking, 1932), see pp. 105 ff.

[39] ST. B. 548. 2. 1. For references to sources see p. 322 in SEBC., and see also pp. 350 ff. The value of Saintyves' article is much diminished by his muddled treatment and his ideas about 'ritual', but it is useful as a source.

[40] iii, 40–43.   [41] AT. 933.

[42] A. W. Wade-Evans, VSB., p. 92.

[43] See SEBC., pp. 323 f.

[44] T. Braga, *Contos Tradicionaes do Povo Portuguez* (Oporto, 1883), no. 142.

[45] The Kentigern tale, though not told specifically of him, was collected as a folktale in Scottish Gaelic in Lochaber a few years ago by the School of Scottish Studies.

[46] But there is a version from Deptford in the *Gentleman's Magazine* for 1765.

[47] In addition to the examples to be traced through the sources mentioned in n. 39, see now also R. Christiansen, FFC., no. 175, pp. 199 ff.

[48] The international folktale called The Grateful Animals (AT. 554, see BP. ii, 19 ff.) includes as one of a series of tasks, to be accomplished before the hero can win a princess, the recovery of a ring or key thrown in the sea; this is done for him by a grateful fish. But this is, of course, not the same story as The Ring of Polycrates at all, though Saintyves treats it as if it were; and, moreover, he gives various instances of AT. 554 without seeming to recognize that they are the same tale. He also includes (though describing them as 'aberrant') examples of still another and different tale, AT. 736.

⁴⁹ *Béaloideas*, viii, 58 f.; cf. ibid. ii, 81 f., versions from Mayo and Ballin-skelligs.

⁵⁰ GS., p. 201.

⁵¹ See BP. in the Abbreviations.

⁵² See TPC. in the Abbreviations.

II

The International Popular Tale: Origin, Diffusion, and Recitation

WHEN we consider the nature of the inter-national popular tale as it was sketched in the previous lecture, the question at once arises, 'What is the origin of this extra-ordinary phenomenon? When did these tales first come into being, and where, and how did they get spread over such vast distances?' Because, as I must emphasize at the start, folklorists nowadays agree that the appearance in so many places of what is obviously one and the same tale cannot be a coincidence. Sometimes, it is true, a story consists of a single episode so simple and univer-sally obvious that it might have arisen quite indepen-dently in a number of separate places—the process called *polygenesis*; but complicated tales like The Magic Flight, and indeed most single-motif ones as well, obviously cannot have done so. They must, therefore, each have originated at some one time and in some one place, and the fact that they appear so often in so many parts of the world is the consequence of diffusion from that centre. There was at one time a school of folklorists who be-lieved that most instances of identity were to be explained as polygenetic; but they were forced to give it up to a large extent, and the idea would have few defenders nowa-days except in the case of very simple motifs.

Various theories have been advanced in the attempt to solve the problem, but most of them suffer from trying to explain too much, from attempting to discover some one simple but striking solution which will account for everything, when the whole matter is really much too complex to yield to such treatment. The question was first asked by the brothers Grimm in 1819.[1] They believed that the international tale was a common property of the Indo-European peoples, inherited from the remote days of Indo-European unity and spread in the course of their migrations in exactly the same way as their Indo-European dialects were spread. But it is rightly objected to this that in that case the subsequent development would have followed the same lines as that of the separate languages did; there would be a definite English type which would be comparatively closely related to the Dutch and German types, and these would be more remotely similar to the Celtic versions, or the Romance, and so on, exactly on the pattern of the relationships of the languages. In the Balkans, Bulgarian and Serbian versions would be much closer to each other than to Albanian or Greek. In fact the situation is not at all like that, and it is not to be explained along Indo-European lines. Besides, there is little doubt that some stories, perhaps a great many, are of more recent origin; and again, the tales are found very widely in areas where the Indo-European people never came. The theory has been revived in a modified form in recent times by Von Sydow,[2] whose ideas seem coloured by the 'Aryan' racial prejudices of the inter-War period, but his very hypothetical arguments fail to carry any conviction. The Grimms believed further that Wonder Tales represent a popular corruption of Indo-European myths about the gods like those we know in Greek, and their followers were not slow to seize on this as a field for delightful speculation about the supposed 'meaning' of a given tale. Since it was generally held at the time that Indo-European religion consisted chiefly of the worship of sky-gods and nature gods, writers like Max Müller[3] and Sir George Cox[4] recklessly interpreted the stories as sun-myths, weather-myths, and so on; and they had considerable influence on Sir John Rhys.[5] This school of thought was hilariously demolished by Andrew Lang[6] and by Henri Gaidoz who proved that Müller was himself a sun-myth by using Müller's own methods.[7] But the sun-gods are still with us, lurking nowadays on the outer fringes of scholarship.

Theodor Benfey the Sanskrit scholar noticed how very often it happens that the oldest traceable version of an international tale is found in Indian literature or in other Oriental sources which are derived from Indian ones. One of the great collections of early Indian popular tales, the *Panchatantra*, which is older than the sixth century A.D., is known to have been translated into Persian in the sixth century, the Persian into Arabic, the Arabic into both Byzantine Greek and Hebrew, and the Hebrew into Latin, so that in this way a number of tales of Indian origin reached Europe. Or again, an Arabic collection of the eighth century called The Book of Sindibad, itself probably derived from India, came to Europe by a similar chain of translations, where it became known as *The Seven Sages of Rome*. I have already spoken of this and have noted the Welsh translation of it in the Red Book of Hergest; and I might mention here that it was in this way that the Oriental story known in this country as the tale of Llywelyn and his faithful hound Gelert[8] reached Wales, not earlier than the fourteenth century. The association with Beddgelert does not ante⁄ date the eighteenth century. Benfey held[9] that almost all types of popular tales had originated in India and had spread to Europe mainly by such written means of trans⁄ mission, beginning for the most part with the tenth cen⁄ tury, though he did admit that oral telling played a minor part before that time. He believed that they also spread eastwards, to Tibet, Mongolia, and China, with the spread of Buddhism. Benfey's theory cannot meet the objection that a considerable number of well⁄known international tales can be shown to have existed in Europe and elsewhere long before the tenth century— Greek sources and the ancient Egyptian stories are in⁄ stances, not to mention early Ireland—and it is now agreed that the history is a great deal less simple than Benfey thought. Nevertheless, it is quite obvious that India was one of the most important homes of the popu⁄ lar tale in early times and must have played a consider⁄ able part in the origin and diffusion of many stories. There is no doubt at all that some tales did reach Europe through the series of translations envisaged by Benfey— Llywelyn and Gelert is an instance.

E. B. Tylor,[10] Andrew Lang,[11] Sir James Frazer,[12] Canon John McCulloch,[13] and others constituted the school of English anthropologists and ritualists. In their view popular tales are an exceedingly ancient expression of the mind of primitive man, and particularly an ex⁄ pression of primitive man's interest in fertility myth and ritual. It was one of their dogmas that primitive man

thinks alike everywhere, and consequently they tended
to emphasize the theory of polygenesis, especially Lang.
The ritualist interpretation held that the stories are to
be understood as myths connected with primitive ritual,
especially fertility rites, just as an earlier generation interpreted them as sun-myths; this was pushed to absurd
extremes by Pierre Saintyves,[14] who was particularly
attached to initiation rituals. There are many objections
to this approach. One trouble is that the anthropologists
did not in the least understand the mind of the modern
and medieval European peasant, in consequence of the
almost impassable gulf which I have already referred to
which has existed in modern times between the educated
urban scholar and the illiterate rural labourer. To treat
the latter, and to interpret his tales and beliefs, as if he
were a savage from Borneo, is completely unrealistic.[15]
Besides, most members of the 'Anthropological school'
paid scant attention to the literary side of the problem and
to the work of men such as Benfey; and they made the
fundamental mistake, made by many others since,[16] of
picking out some one version of a story which they
happened to know, or which might be made to suit their
theories, and arguing from this, instead of first taking the
indispensable step of collecting all possible versions and
submitting them to comparative criticism. In addition,
they made a great deal too much of the supposed primitive character of the folktale. This theory has long been
discredited so far as the serious up-to-date international
study of the folktale is concerned.

By far the most important and soundest contribution
to the study and interpretation of the popular tale is provided by the work of the so-called 'Finnish' school, a

group of scholars of whom the earliest were Finns and the majority of others Scandinavians until their views won the wide acceptance which, with modifications, is now accorded them—a school pioneered by men such as Julius and Karl Krohn and Antti Aarne.[17] These scholars worked out the so-called 'historic-geographic' method, which consists first of collecting every known version of the tale which is being studied and ranging them chronologically and geographically, and then attempting by the standard principles of comparative criticism to arrive at what must have been the *original* form which will account for all the variants, and to discover where and when this original form came into existence and by what routes it migrated. Only when a large number of such comparative studies had been made did the Finns feel it would be possible to arrive at a general theory. Their work has in fact already shown that the places of origin of various tales are very various, and that no one sweeping exclusive hypothesis can stand. Ancient India was certainly one very important source, but there were others too, including notably medieval western Europe. Also the dates when different stories arose may vary widely; some are very ancient, others are more recent, some much more recent, but in their view none are really *primitive*—it is one of their doctrines that 'the folktale is a product of civilisation'. As regards dissemination, they worked out what is called the 'ripple theory', that is, that stories were spread by a slow process of one man telling them to, as it were, his next-door neighbour, so that they gradually extended in ever-widening concentric circles without any movement of population, just as the ripples on a pool spread outwards without the water itself moving in a centrifugal direction. This theory was constructed to suit the rather special situation of rural Finland in the nineteenth century; it does not apply at all well to world conditions over the centuries since the beginning of civilization, and most folklorists nowadays would scarcely subscribe to it. It has been objected to the Finnish school, with some justice, that they have not been very interested in literary popular tales and particularly in their transmission by literary means, and that they have devoted their attention too exclusively to the folk versions and to oral transmission.[18] Nevertheless, by and large the Finnish theory and method has marked an epoch in the history of the study of the folktale; it has put out of date everything that went before, and all future work must reckon with its premises.

Having summarized briefly the main theories which have dominated the field of folklore research for the last century and a half, I should like to put before you a view of the origin and spread of the popular tale which I hope may be felt to be reasonable. In the first place, I do not believe that it is necessary to *account* for its existence, whether by supposing it to represent the detritus of old myths, or the expression of rituals, or the dreams of hashish-eaters and others (as has been suggested). Such hypotheses are dangerous attempts to be too clever—dangerous because they invariably lead to their author's attempting to force the facts to fit the theory. No explanation is needed, it seems to me, other than the fact that man has always loved stories and story-telling for their own sake as entertainment and always will love them for that reason. This is a universal human activity, and does not require to be accounted for. Secondly, I agree with practically all modern folklorists that for any but the most simple and obvious themes, polygenesis will not do. The complex story such as The Magic Flight or hun, dreds of others, and the simple but striking and extra, ordinary tale like The Ring of Polycrates, cannot have arisen independently in different parts of the world, and they must, therefore, each have had one single origin in one single place at one single time, and must have spread from that centre by diffusion. I am perfectly convinced that the popular tales of the European and Asiatic type as we know them are not genuinely *primitive*, do not go back to the savage days of Paleolithic man. Certainly there are elements, such as the Life Token, the External Soul, and so on, in some types, the Wonder Tale in particular, which do seem primitive and do have striking echoes among the beliefs of savage peoples— though I think both their frequency and their primitive, ness has often been exaggerated. But this is not to say that the period when our tales were composed was necessarily a primitive one. These things, I suggest, were picturesque, ancient superstitions, such as would only naturally be used by the composers of entertaining tales of magic, exactly as we bring witches and fairies and the rest into the tales we invent to tell our own children. After all, the English and Scottish Border Ballads are full of exactly the same sort of so,called primitive motifs, frequently the identical ones, that we find in the Wonder Tales, and we all know that these poems were composed in the late medieval period and later.[19] Some tales, no doubt, are demonstrably *ancient*, such as the Egyptian story of The Two Brothers or the Greek myth of Perseus and the Monster, but the Finns are, I think, certainly right to treat them as the product of comparatively civilized man. One reason is that a large number of our popular inter⁄ national tales are genuine works of art, the work of men with truly civilized and artistic minds, with involved, complicated, but very logically constructed plots; noth⁄ ing could be more unlike the popular tales of genuine savage peoples as we know them at the present day. This is a point to which I shall return.

Further, the origin of our international popular tales is, I believe, most certainly not to be looked for in any one place exclusively; no doubt the practice of telling them first grew up in several centres of ancient civilization, perhaps all. India was unquestionably one, but so were ancient Sumeria and Babylonia, Egypt and Greece, and in later times western Europe. The oral diffusion of these stories must have been carried on from the beginning in a great variety of ways—the Finnish 'ripple' theory is quite inadequate. Certainly, migrations of whole peoples would be one obvious way—so far the Grimms were right—but the movements of individuals must also have had a great deal to do with it. It is well known that travelling men, beggars, tinkers, and so on, have played a large part in the diffusion of tales in Ireland, as is proved by the evidence of contemporary witnesses,[20] and there is no reason at all why the same should not have been the case in ancient and medieval times in many parts of Europe and Asia. Travel for the purposes of trade and the like has been carried on since civilization began, from the wandering copper⁄smiths at the beginning of the Bronze Age and the amber merchants on the ancient route from the Baltic to Greece, down to the medieval pilgrims and Crusaders and the modern colonists of the

New World. In fact stories like Cinderella found in the Americas were, of course, taken there by colonists. Again, conditions during the Roman Empire were ideal for the diffusion of stories; extending from Persia to Spain and Scotland and from North Africa to Germany, and with the constant recruiting of soldiers in one area and their posting to some other area at the other end of the Roman world, not to mention the traffic in slaves, the journeys of merchants and traders, and the rest, the Empire must have done a great deal to further the wide dissemination of early popular tales. I would ask you to remember this in connexion with their appearance in Wales. Finally, the Jewish Diaspora in the first century A.D. would certainly be a factor, for the part played in the transmission of many types of story by the Jews, and especially as a bridge between Orient and Occident, has been a large one, and would repay study.

We must not forget diffusion by the written word. I have quoted the *Panchatantra* and the Book of Sindibad as examples of eastern literary collections which became popular in Europe by means of a chain of written trans-lations, but there were others too; and further, the same process took a great many Indian tales to central Asia and the Far East under the impulse of Buddhism. We must remember also the constant borrowing of individual tales by literary men from one another, as from Boccaccio by Chaucer, such tales often eventually reaching the illiterate peasantry. From at least the beginning of the Middle Ages in Europe, down to the eighteenth- and early nineteenth-century popularity of the chap-book, with its stories from the Arabian Nights, from the *Gesta Romanorum*, from the romances of medieval chivalry, and scores of others, hawked around the countryside of Europe by pedlars, the written and printed word has been an immensely important factor in the diffusion of the popular tale. Once again let me stress what I have emphasized before, the constant two-way traffic in the popular tale between literature and folklore; as well as the vastness of this great body of narrative and the extra-ordinary indestructibility of the individual tale.

There are three further points I should like to make about the study of the international popular tale at this stage. First, I would remark that in studying some tale or motif it is absolutely essential to examine the great mass of material made available by the Aarne–Thompson and Stith Thompson indexes, Bolte and Polivka, and the works of the Finnish school on individual stories. There is no excuse nowadays for ignoring the fact that many other versions of the story with which one is concerned probably exist in many languages, not merely in the lan-guage in which one is interested, and are easily available. Further, it is a disastrous mistake to confine one's com-parative study to one or two other versions, very likely quite aberrant and untypical, which one happens to know—more particularly if they seem to suit one's theory. It is necessary if possible to discover the *original* form of the tale, as well as the history of the modifications it has undergone in the more immediate area concerned. To pick some one version at random, ignoring the rest of the whole field, is no longer permissible.

Secondly, it is very unwise to let one's investigations be coloured by some preconceived favourite theory of origins, whether mythological, ritualistic, or anything else. It is unwise because it almost inevitably leads to attempts to twist the material to suit the theory in trying to interpret the 'meaning' of the tale. For instance, in his most recent work W. J. Gruffydd revived the old notion that the fairies are nothing but a memory of a primitive dwarfish Stone Age or Bronze Age human population, driven to live in the wilds by the more powerful and physically larger immigrant users of iron—a theory which has long ago been abandoned by folklorists. He applied this to the motif of the Lady of the Lake in the Meddygon Myddfai legend. In this tale a man has to pick out his proposed bride from two women who look exactly alike, but one of them gives him a sign with her foot and he rightly chooses her. Gruffydd seeks to explain this by saying that the Little People must have all seemed very much alike to their Iron Age supplanters (in much the same way, I suppose, as Europeans often say that all Chinese look the same to them); and he used this as a piece of evidence to support a theory.[21] But in fact this motif of the choice of a certain woman out of a number of others who look exactly alike, which is successfully made because she gives some signal to the hero or has on her some token known only to her and to him, is a very wide-spread and well-recognized international one, duly cata-logued in Thompson's Motif-Index.[22] It belongs in particular to three familiar international wonder-tales, The Magic Flight, The Magician and his Pupil,[23] and The Grateful Animals;[24] we have already seen it in the Indian version of The Magic Flight where Sringabhuja successfully chose the demon's daughter from among her hundred identical sisters because she wore her necklace differently from them; but the usual thing is that the dis-guised person makes a sign with hand or foot, as in the

Meddygon Myddfai. The Lady of the Lake, or The Water-Fairy Bride, is, of course, another familiar international tale, and the Meddygon Myddfai version of it is the only instance known to me anywhere of the association of the recognition motif with it, even among Welsh versions; so that it is obvious that this association is secondary and quite fortuitous. Possibly Gruffydd's theory may be allowed to be cancelled out by Von Sydow's, who takes the recognition motif for part of a primitive marriage ritual, and Von Sydow's by Gruffydd's![25]

Thirdly, if the discussion of the international popular tale, both oral and literary, in these lectures so far has shown anything, it has shown that a large number of versions of a given tale may exist; that very many more may once have existed but have never been recorded; and that therefore we must of necessity take it for granted that our record is very incomplete. It follows that when we are dealing with literatures in which oral telling is known or believed with good reason to have played a very large part, we ought not to assume that some particular version known to us—call it B—of any given story is *directly* derived from version A unless there is some definite and irrefutable piece of evidence other than identity of plot to prove that version B does actually come directly from version A and not from some third version now lost. B may indeed be close to A, perhaps very close, but where oral transmission has been an important aspect of a literature it is clear in logic and common sense that the assumption of the lost common source must necessarily prevail, or at least it is impossible to assert the opposite in the absence of very strong reason to the contrary. (Of

course, with literatures in which the transmission has
been solely by means of writing, and therefore much
more limited, the problem may be different and it may
be much easier to trace the history of a tale.) It is unlucky
that convincing evidence of direct derivation is hard to
come by; though if there is some really quite extraordinary perversion of the plot found in two versions
only it does at least create a strong presumption of a very
close connexion of some sort, providing there is enough
other material to show that it *is* a perversion of the norm.
Particular versions of stories not infrequently show
internal evidence of their place of immediate origin.
Thus the international tale of the soldier who excuses his
playing cards in church by explaining the pack as a holy
calendar and prayerbook[26] was told in England of one
Richard Middleton.[27] The French version which likewise makes the hero Richard Middleton[28] is therefore
obviously of English origin and doubtless recent; but
this does not identify for us the actual English *version*
from which the French one came, as he is Richard
Middleton in several existing English ones and no doubt
was so in many others now lost. Since the original
authors of the international popular tales are no longer
alive we cannot interrogate them, and are not in the
position of a friend of mine who many years ago, when
we were both undergraduates at Cambridge, himself composed and told his friends a Limerick about the Bishop
of Bath and Wells. A couple of years later he went
to America as a research student, and he was thunder-
struck when there to be told his own Limerick by a Yale
man, and told it as an example of American humour!
In this case the mention of Bath and Wells would

doubtless betray its English origin, but the actual author himself knew where in England it had really come from. Unfortunately this cannot happen now when we are investigating the history of the traditional popular tale.

I should like to turn our attention now to some discussion of the people who preserve and tell the popular oral tale, and to some aspects of their art. This is a subject on which there has been a good deal of misunderstanding because it was in the past such a rare thing for the scholar to know anything at all at first hand about the social group he calls the 'Folk'. I have already remarked that there is very little excuse for this in the British Isles; it is not necessary to go to Serbia or Siberia to study the folktale teller or singer of heroic narrative poetry in action, since it is still done much more easily by a visit to the west of Ireland or Scotland. Here there are still expert folktale tellers of great artistic skill whose tradition reaches back to the Middle Ages and beyond, and one can therefore study their craft as a living thing in a living community. This must be done on the spot, and it is indispensable not merely to the folklorist but also to any student of early and medieval comparative literature if he handles material of a popular nature like the Mabinogion.

What kind of people are these story-tellers? They represent the intelligentsia of the old rural Gaelic tradition; men of high intelligence, with keen minds and memories sharpened by practice, devoted to stories and legends, the enthusiastic guardians of their inherited oral Gaelic literature, and true artists in their craft. They are men widely educated in the old oral learning of their people, though generally illiterate in their own language and not infrequently in English as well, at any rate until recent times. They play, or used to play, a highly important part in the life of their community because they were the focus of its intellectual activity; they held a sort of unofficial position as if unpaid professional men, which gave them a standing in the neighbourhood. Let me quote from J. H. Delargy:[29]

In every townland in the district there was at least one house to which, as a rule, the same literary clientele would resort during the nights of winter, usually from mid-September to 17 March; but the story-telling did not really start until *Oidhche Shamhna* (31 October). Ó Heochaidh points out that the old story-tellers seemed to be loth to tell folk-tales in their own homes, and would rather go to a *toigh áirneáil* [a house where story-telling was practised] than tell their tales in the presence of their own families. In the congenial atmosphere of the house of story-telling, un-disturbed by the noise and prattle of children, their sensitive artistry was appreciated by the grown-up audience, mainly men, for whom these tales were intended. In return for the hospitality of the occupiers the guests attended to their simple wants, bringing turf from the stack, water from the well, and helping in various ways to put the house in order. The stage was soon set for the story-teller, a blazing turf fire provided the light, a stool or chair of the householder's slender store was assigned to him in the place of honour beside the fire; and here he awaited the arrival of the visitors; some of these were old men like himself who had been preparing, perhaps for hours before, for the night's entertainment. . . . When the house was full to the door, the man of the house would fill his pipe with tobacco, and give it to the most respected guest. The person thus favoured smoked it for a while, then handed it back to its owner; after that it went round the company from one to another. By the time the last man had had his smoke, all the current topics of interest had been discussed, and the story telling could now begin.

Delargy says elsewhere,[30] of a travelling man who was a story-teller:

At one of his 'stage-houses' . . . he used to tell stories every night until 2 a.m. for a whole week at a time. Diarmuid would choose his night quarters with some deliberation. On his arrival, he used to take his place at the head of the kitchen table, where, glass in hand, sipping at his drink, with his admirers gathered round him, he awaited the arrival of others who had been apprised of his coming. The house soon filled up . . .; those for whom there was no seat leaned up against the walls, and in the silence before the tale began there was no sound save the crackle of the fire and the chirp of the cricket. Diarmuid Ó Sé must have been a master story-teller, for over a wide area from which we have obtained many hundreds of tales, the memory of his skill still lingers.

Delargy adds the words of a man who remembered this story-teller when he was a boy:

The other boys thought I was too young to go with them to the house where Diarmuid was staying, but I would give them the slip, and would hide under the kitchen table, where I could listen to the tales, undisturbed. There is not a word the story-teller would say that I had not off by heart the next morning.

The situation was the same in Gaelic Scotland. J. F. Campbell of Islay quotes a good description of it in Wester Ross given him in 1860:[31]

When I was a boy, it was the custom for the young to assemble together on the long winter nights to hear the old people recite the tales or *sgeulachd* which they had learned from their fathers before them. In those days tailors and shoe⁄makers went from house to house, making our clothes and shoes. . . . I knew an old tailor who used to tell a new tale every night during his stay in the village. . . . It was also the custom when a . . . stranger, celebrated for his store of tales, came on a visit to the village, for us, young and old, to make a rush to the house where he passed the night, and choose our seats . . . and listen in silence to the new tales. . . . The goodman of the house usually opened with the tale of . . . [the] great giant or some other favourite tale, and the stranger carried on after that. It was a common saying, 'The first tale by the goodman, and tales to daylight by the . . . guest'.[32]

I can vouch for it myself that the state of affairs de⁄scribed by Delargy in Ireland was still in existence when I used to stay on the Blasket Island in West Kerry and listen to Peig Sayers tell her tales in the evenings to the company that gathered there to hear her. In Nova Scotia and in Scotland, in more recent years, I have not been present myself when any number of people have come together to listen to tellers, and have done my collecting of tales alone with them. As a matter of fact the practice, as a formal social occasion, seems to be extinct in Scot⁄land nowadays. At any rate the tellers are still there, though reduced to few. Incidentally, these passages which I have quoted, and others like them, bring out the fact that tale⁄telling was not done for the benefit of the child⁄ren but for that of the grown⁄ups, chiefly the men. This is, of course, universally the case; the folktale is intended as the entertainment of adults, not children.

The *public* function of the story⁄teller in the com⁄munity is the clue to the whole phenomenon; he is, or was, the wireless and television, the theatre and cinema, and public library of the village. A good prose style and a good delivery were much appreciated—indeed, so far as it is possible for a man sitting in a chair, the story-teller *acts* his story; and one teller I knew, Niall Gillies of Castlebay in Barra, used to jump up and stride about the room, swinging his arms and declaiming, when he reached a particularly exciting passage. Tadhg Ó Murchú, one of Delargy's collectors, describes a Kerry man in action as follows:

His piercing eyes are on my face, his limbs are trembling, as, immersed in his story, and forgetful of all else, he puts his very soul into the telling. Obviously much affected by his narrative, he uses a great deal of gesticulation, and by the move-ment of his body, hands, and head, tries to convey hate and anger, fear and humour, like an actor in a play. He raises his voice at certain passages, at other times it becomes almost a whisper. He speaks fairly fast, but his enunciation is at all times clear. I have never met anyone who told his tales with more artistry and effect than this very fine old story-teller.[33]

So far so good; but how do these people manage to remember and preserve such large numbers of long stories in the way they do? For some of them know hundreds of tales, many of great length—the Scottish Gaelic tale The Healing of Cian's Leg is over 30,000 words in the version from Islay collected for J. F. Camp-bell[34]—and some very striking instances are recorded of tellers who could memorize long tales they had only heard once, and repeat them almost word for word.[35] The answer is a complex one. In the first place, they are of course men of intelligence with naturally good mem-ories, and moreover are intensely interested in their favourite pursuit and hence can remember stories much more easily than if this was a boring labour to them. Then, constant telling kept them in practice—Delargy quotes the case of one who kept his tales fresh in his mind by repeating them aloud to himself when the local people had lost interest and he could no longer command an audience.[36] Finally, the listeners themselves play an important part in the preservation of the tradition. They have often heard the tale before (though they are none the less eager for that reason to hear it again), and if the teller makes a mistake or is at a loss they can correct him and put him on the track again, and indeed often do so. Thus people who are not themselves capable of reciting tales may nevertheless do much to keep them intact.

But there is another and highly important factor responsible for what I have called the 'indestructibility' of the popular tale; stories that have survived for centuries have obviously done this because they are adapted to do so. The complex tale as we know it in Europe and Asia has an exceedingly tight-knit plot. It holds itself together almost automatically because of the logic of its interlocking construction, in which episode 3 is a necessary and foreseeable consequence of episode 2, and episode 2 of episode 1, and so on, and the whole thing is pulled together neatly at the end with the resolution of the problem. Such a story is not easily forgotten. An example is The Magic Flight, which I have already treated as the paradigm of the international popular tale at its best. It tells first how the hero comes into the power of the ogre and meets his daughter; then the tasks are set him and performed in due order with the help of the girl; the couple escape, pursued by the ogre, but delay and finally baffle him either by throwing objects behind them, or by transforming themselves, or both (both usually in threes); arrived home, the hero forgets the girl because he breaks a magic prohibition and is about to marry another, but the heroine brings herself to mind by magic means; and the whole is rounded off by the happy ending of their wedding. This complicated tale is skil-fully and beautifully told by a good teller, and in fact any teller at all worth his salt can preserve without difficulty and without serious corruption both this and scores, even hundreds, of others; and the reason is partly the reciter's own innate qualities of intelligence, memory, and interest, as well as the co-operation of his audience where neces-sary, and partly the intrinsic character of the material he uses.

The folktales of present-day savage peoples are a very different matter. They seem to lack any real *construction* whatsoever. They take a character, such as the 'Cotton-tail' of the American Indians, and describe his adven-tures, but these meander on from one to the next without any logic, without any co-ordination and sub-ordination, entirely without plot, just like the efforts at story-telling of a child. Hence they are very much more difficult to remember, and rapidly fall to pieces, so that it is not easy to recognize a given version as being essentially 'the same' as another. The Cambridge psychologist F. C. Bartlett conducted an interesting experiment in studying the remembering of folktales some years ago.[37] He had a group of students read an American Indian folktale, and then repeat it to him after the lapse of certain fixed intervals of time, beginning with 15 minutes. His conclusions about remembering and forgetting are of

great interest, though they are too lengthy to be sum
marized here; but there are two factors about this experi
ment which make it of little relevance to the situation
that I am discussing. In the first place, the tale was a
savage one, not a civilized one, and consequently was
lacking in the logical internal construction I have de
scribed. The choice was deliberate on Bartlett's part, but
it was unfortunate in a way because it reduces the value
of his conclusions in respect of the folktale in Europe and
Asia. Secondly, his students were not professional folk
tale tellers, habituated to seizing the essential plot of a
story heard for the first time. Hence, though Bartlett's
results are most interesting as a scientific experimental
study of memory, they are not as useful to the student of
the European-Asiatic folktale as one could wish. A
much less valuable experiment was conducted by Albert
Wesselski.[38] Wesselski knew the literary aspects of the
popular tale as few have ever known them, but he was
quite ignorant of the living folktale and was positively
hostile to the idea that stories can be handed on success
fully by word of mouth—he was a fine example of the
cloistered scholar with absolutely no understanding of
the peasant. His experiment was designed to prove his
case. He took a class of Sudeten German schoolgirls,
aged 12 to 13, and had read to them the story of The Sleep
ing Beauty, which they then had to write out. They did it
very badly, and many obviously did not remember even
the essential features, or at any rate could not get them
down on paper. From this Wesselski concluded that
tales simply cannot *be* remembered and handed on by
word of mouth—the testimony of over a century of folk
tale recording notwithstanding. Of course, Wesselski's

'experiment' was worthless; folktale tellers are not little schoolgirls aged 12 to 13, and besides if there are any school-teachers in the present audience I dare say they may agree with me that some of the girls may really have remembered the tale a great deal better than they could express on paper.

All this is not to say, of course, that folktale tellers do not sometimes forget stories or parts of them, and hand them on in a corrupted fashion. Naturally they may; and the conditions of this forgetting and corruption have been studied by the Finnish folklorists.[39] In the hands of an unskilful teller some essential clue may go astray; the next teller who learns it from him has then lost the thread; and unless he cleverly patches it, perhaps pro-ducing a new sub-version which will develop a life of its own, the whole story soon becomes unrecognizable and pointless and goes to pieces. Thus, the oral tradition of the popular tale has a built-in self defence—these un-desirable 'mutations' quickly die out because they are not equipped to live, and it is not Gresham's Law but Dar-win's 'Survival of the Fittest' that rules the popular tale.

I want to give one or two examples of this deteriora-tion in practice, because it will be significant for what I shall have to say about Welsh. My first is the tale The Magician and his Pupil,[40] a story exceedingly popular in Europe (including Ireland and Scotland), and in Asia, and probably of Indian origin; it occurs in Europe first in Straparola's sixteenth-century Italian *Piacevole Notti*.[41] I will summarize in some detail a good and representa-tive version of it that I got from Peig Sayers,[42] as I shall return to this story in a later lecture. A magician offers to teach a fisherman's son magic, but will not let him go when the three years bargained for are up. The father asks for him back, and is told he can have him if he can recognize him among eleven other pupils; and when he is confronted with them, they are magically in the form of ducks. However, the boy makes a prearranged signal and the father chooses the right duck (here is our friend the recognition motif again, supposed by Gruffydd to refer to the indistinguishability of the Little People). Boy and father flee in the shape of hawks and are pursued by eleven other hawks; the boy appeals for help to a girl and changes himself into a ring on her finger. The eleven pupils arrive and demand the ring, but the girl throws it into a barn full of corn, and while they are seeking it among the grains in the form of wild ducks the boy escapes in the guise of a flea. Next, both having got safely away, he arranges that he shall change himself to a horse and his father shall sell him to the magician, and, when the money has been paid over, shall remove the bridle and the horse will vanish. This is done success⁄fully once, but when they try to repeat the trick the father forgets the bridle and the magician rides the horse away, spurring it cruelly. However, the horse succeeds in ridding itself of the bridle by a trick while drinking at a stream, changes itself to an eel, and escapes. The tale should end with a mutual transformation combat between the boy and the magician, in which the boy as a fox finally bites off the head of the magician in the shape of a bird, but in this version Peig Sayers has changed it slightly to a mere test of skill between the boy and a friendly wizard—in itself an example of how motifs may inadvertently be changed. However, the point at the moment is the contrast of this with a corrupt version which has also gained some currency in Ireland, in which a man who wants his son to marry is told by the father of the prospective bride that none but a craftsman will do, and hands him on to the magician to learn magic. The magician refuses to let him go, as before, and the father comes to his house to fetch him, but the magician then gives him up without more ado; there is none of the recognition motif or the transformation flight. The episode of selling the horse follows, but not the failure to remember the bridle; and the story ends at this point with father and son going to the girl's house and the son making a magic mansion on wheels, by which means he wins the girl.[43] Here, large essential parts of the tale have dropped out, and it is mutilated in consequence. The version collected in Germany by the Brothers Grimm and published as their no. 68 is not much better.

We all know the story of Snow White.[44] It is familiar throughout Europe and the Near East, and is found already in the *Pentamerone* of Basile in the seventeenth century. The plot is that her stepmother learns that Snow White is more beautiful than she is, and she orders her huntsman to bring her Snow White's heart, but the merciful man substitutes an animal's heart and lets her go in the forest. She is rescued by the dwarfs; the stepmother discovers this and tries three times to poison her. The dwarfs revive her twice but fail the third time, and keep her in a glass coffin. A prince sees her, and resuscitates and marries her, and the stepmother is punished. Now, a version of this tale from Kerry[45] has lost the motif that the stepdaughter is more beautiful and has also lost the episodes about the rescue by the dwarfs and the attempted poisonings. Instead, the prince discovers the girl in a wood and makes her one of his servants. Later he wants to marry, and institutes a test of chastity for the candidates, but the girl is the only one to pass it, and they are married. Her friendly stepsister tells her the stepmother is dead. This version of Snow White has obviously become very corrupted by incompetent telling; it has forgotten some essential parts and has added a lame ending which does not belong to the tale.

This sort of thing does not often happen with good story-tellers. But when a person who is not a story-teller at all attempts to tell one, corruption of this kind is particularly common, because he lacks the trained memory and the skill and experience to grasp the plot and retain the essentials. It is notable that when philologists writing phonetic descriptions of dialects give phonetically transcribed folktales as specimens of the dialect, such tales are very often short, corrupt, and feeble; the reason being that the informant with whom the student worked had naturally been picked not because he was a skilled story-teller but because he was particularly suitable for linguistic study. For example, the tale of Tom Thumb[46] tells how a childless couple wish for a child no matter how small, and they have a boy the size of a thumb. A considerable series of adventures and misadventures follows, all turning on the point of his small size. A version of this in Holmer's study on the Irish dialect of Rathlin Island[47] has forgotten the opening motif about the wish and the child the size of a thumb, though it preserves a version of the name,[48] and has only one of the adventures to tell—how the child was swallowed by a cow and rescued. The whole thing is only 100 words in length. Clearly this was told by an amateur who had never had any experience as a story-teller, but had heard the tale and remembered parts of it. It is a good illustration of the fact that corruption is especially rapid and thorough when stories are handled by someone who is not a professional. The significance of this for the Welsh material will appear later.

One way in which even the experienced teller may change the form of a tale is by combination. He may string two separate stories together and make them one. For instance, when Peig Sayers told me the version of The Magician and his Pupil just summarized, she made the hero's adventures continue with a completely different one, that known in Ireland as *Gabha an tSuic*,[49] The Smith of the Ploughshare. Or, the splendid story from the Argyll roadmender referred to in my first lecture consists of The Princess and the Riddles[50] to which The Ogre's External Soul[51] has been added, and this is not due to incompetence, since the teller was a master craftsman. This kind of thing is especially common with certain classes of humorous tale. Or, one story may be interpolated into the middle of the other. So, The Dragon Slayer or Perseus story is commonly found inserted into quite a different tale, The Two Brothers, at the point where the elder twin comes to the far country and is to get a wife. This 'mutation' is ancient, and was fortunate enough to catch on, so that it has become as it were a tale in its own right with a wide distribution.[52] There is a version of this conflate story in J. F. Campbell's *Popular Tales of the West Highlands*[53] into which still another separate tale has been interpolated, The Ogre's External Soul, or more strictly speaking The Dragon Slayer has been interpolated into The Ogre's External Soul and this conflate into The Two Brothers. Nor is this a mere freak, the whimsy of the teller himself, since Campbell gives two other versions of the same very conflate tale, though less complete because they lack the last part of The Two Brothers, from other parts of the Highlands. In this sort of way compound 'mutations' may arise, but they are not very common and usually do not survive.

NOTES TO LECTURE II

[1] See *Kinder- und Hausmärchen* (Leipzig, 1856), iii, 427 ff.

[2] C. W. von Sydow, *Das Märchen als indogermanische Tradition*; Nieder-deutsche Zeitschrift für Volkskunde, iv (1926), 207 ff. See criticisms in the *American Journal of Folklore*, xliv, no. 171 (1931), 54 ff.; and by Krohn in FFC., no. 96 (1931), pp. 6 ff. Von Sydow's views were re-stated in *Das Volksmärchen unter ethnischem Gesichtspunkt*, in *Essays and Studies Presented to Professor Eoin MacNeill* (ed. J. Ryan, Dublin, 1940), pp. 567 ff., and in VF., pp. 15 ff.

[3] 'Comparative Mythology', in *Oxford Essays*, 1856 (London, 1856), pp. 1 ff.; *Chips From a German Workshop* (London, 1867–75); *Selected Essays on Language, Mythology, and Religion* (London, 1881).

[4] *Mythology of the Aryan Nations* (London, 1870).

[5] Cf., for example, *Lectures on the Origin and Growth of Religion* (Hibbert Lects., 1886; London, 1888), pp. 383 ff.

[6] Introduction to Margaret Hunt's *Grimm's Household Tales* (London, 1892).

[7] *Mélusine*, ii, 73 ff.   [8] ST. B. 331. 2.

[9] See his *Pantschatantra* (Leipzig, 1859).

[10] *Primitive Culture* (London, 1891).

[11] Introduction to Hunt's *Grimm* cited above, n. 6; *Custom and Myth* (London, 1884); *Myth, Ritual, and Religion* (2nd ed., London, 1889).

[12] *The Golden Bough*, 3rd ed., 12 vols. (London, 1907–15); *Folklore in the Old Testament* (London, 1918).

[13] *The Childhood of Fiction* (London, 1905).

[14] *Les Contes de Perrault et les récits parallèles* (Paris, 1923), &c.

[15] Compare A. H. Krappe, *The Science of Folk-Lore* (London, 1930), pp. xvii ff.

[16] Notably those writers who try to explain the folktale on psychological lines.

[17] For an account of the Finnish school and its methods see A. Aarne, *Leitfaden der vergleichenden Märchenforschung*, FFC., no. 13; K. Krohn, *Die folkloristische Arbeitsmethode* (Oslo, 1926); id., *Übersicht über einige Resultate der Märchenforschung*, FFC., no. 96; S. Thompson, *The Folktale since Basile*, in N. M. Penzer, *The Pentamerone of Basile* (London, 1932), ii, 287 ff.; id., *The Folktale* (New York, 1946), pp. 428 ff.; A. Taylor, *Precursors of the Finnish Method of Folklore Study*, in *Modern Philology*, xxv, 481 ff.; E. J. Lindgren, *The Collection and Analysis of Folklore*, in *The Study of Society* (ed. F. C. Bartlett and others, London, 1939), chap. xiv.

[18] Cf. A. Wesselski, *Märchen des Mittelalters* (Berlin, 1925); and VTM. (see Abbreviations). The theories of Wesselski are, however, themselves highly complicated and unsatisfactory; and cf. W. Anderson, *Zu Albert*

Wesselskis Angriffen auf die finnische folkloristische Arbeitsmethode (Commen-
tationes Archivi Traditionum Popularium Estoniae; Dorpat, 1935).

[19] On this point see some sage remarks by G. H. Gerould in *The Ballad
of Tradition* (Oxford, 1932), pp. 151 f.

[20] Cf., for example, Delargy, GS., pp. 198 ff.

[21] W. J. Gruffydd, *Folklore and Myth in the Mabinogion* (Cardiff, 1950),
pp. 10 f.

[22] ST. H. 324, and its variant H. 161.

[23] AT. 325.   [24] AT. 554.

[25] VF., p. 78.   [26] AT. 1613.

[27] See Edward Wilson in *Folklore*, l, 263 ff.

[28] See *Zeitschrift des Vereins für Volkskunde*, xi, 377.

[29] GS., p. 193. I wish to thank Professor Delargy most cordially for
generously allowing me to quote this long passage, and the others which
follow, from his lecture.

[30] Op. cit., p. 199.   [31] TWH. I, xiv f.

[32] I should like to draw attention also to the vivid description of what he
calls 'an Irish concert' by Martin Freeman in the *Journal of the Folk-Song
Society*, vi, no. 23 (1920), pp. xxi ff.

[33] GS., p. 190.

[34] See TGSI. xxv, 189 ff. Delargy refers to an Irish tale of about 34,000
words collected in Connemara; GS., p. 190.

[35] Cf. GS., pp. 201, 208.   [36] GS., p. 186.

[37] In his book *Remembering* (Cambridge, 1950), pp. 63 ff.

[38] VTM., pp. 127 ff.

[39] See A. Aarne, *Leitfaden der vergleichenden Märchenforschung*, FFC., no.
13, pp. 23 ff.; K. Krohn, *Die folkloristische Arbeitsmethode* (Institutet for
Sammenlignende Kulturforskning, Oslo, 1926, Serie B, v), pp. 59 ff.

[40] AT. 325; see BP. ii, 60 ff.   [41] viii, 5.

[42] *Béaloideas*, viii, 3 ff.

[43] An Seabhac, *An Seanchaidhe Muimhneach* (Dublin, 1932), no. 27, from
Ballyferriter; cf. Douglas Hyde, *Leabhar Sgeulaigheachta* (Dublin, 1889), pp.
149 ff., from Ballinrobe.

[44] AT. 709; see BP. i, 450 ff.   [45] *Béaloideas*, ii, 274 ff.

[46] AT. 700; see BP. i, 389 ff.

[47] N. Holmer, *The Irish Language in Rathlin Island, Co. Antrim*; RIA. Todd
Lecture Series, xviii (1942), p. 152; compare the folktales in T. de Bhald-
raithe's *The Irish of Cois Fhairrge, Co. Galway* (Dublin, 1945), pp. 72 ff.

[48] *Súil Órdóige*.

[49] AT. 753, see BP. ii, 198 ff., and O. Bergin and C. Marstrander, *Mis-
cellany Presented to Kuno Meyer* (Halle, 1912), pp. 371 ff.

[50] AT. 851, see BP. i, 188 ff.

[51] AT. 302, see BP. iii, 434 ff.

[52] See the study on this by K. Ranke, *Die Zwei Brüder*, FFC., no. 114.

[53] TWH. i, no. 4, 'The Sea Maiden'.

III

The International Popular Tale in Early Wales: 1

IN this and the following lecture I am now going to discuss instances of international popular tales which occur in early Welsh literature. In the course of doing so, I shall continually be quoting parallels to Welsh tales in all kinds of other literatures and folk-lores, some of them belonging to countries very remote from Wales, Sanskrit collections or the Arabian Nights for example, or not known to occur in sources so early as the Welsh. If anyone thinks such things too remote to have any relevance to early Wales, however, and is sceptical about the international character of the Welsh instances and the view that this internationality includes Wales, I shall have failed entirely in what I set out to do in the first two lectures. Of course, every suggested instance must be judged on its own merits, but by and large the great mass of international popular tale includes Wales as it does the rest of Europe—it would be very odd if it did not. I have already suggested that many international motifs may have reached Wales during the period of the Roman Empire, but some may well have been there before that—if we believe the Grimms and Von Sydow, of course, it would be very long before that. The fact that the examples of international motifs which occur in sources like the *Four Branches*, dating from the late eleventh century, are very early is something I should like to emphasize, because most folklorists, and especially perhaps those of the Finnish school, seem to have failed in a rather curious way to realize that Ireland and Wales between them not infrequently provide very old instances of a given tale or motif, sometimes the oldest known. This is due to the fact that the Celtic literatures are so old and so rich in story-telling, that international tales appear in them which did not get recorded in other countries till much later. Folklorists are usually not Celtic scholars, but the way they often seem to be quite unaware of this vital fact is surprising. They may quote examples from the *Four Branches* and yet treat this as if it was on a parallel with a modern collection of folktales.

Perhaps some people have been saying to themselves already, 'This is all very fine, but what reason have we to suppose that international tales and motifs had in fact reached Wales early enough to be incorporated in material like the Mabinogion?' If so, I hope to persuade them shortly, by actual examples, that they had. But first, the case would be strengthened *a priori* if it can be shown that they are found as early as this in other parts of the British Isles. There is not room to dilate on this subject in these lectures, but I may mention briefly two or three examples in early Irish which will show that they are. I have already noted that The Ring of Polycrates is in Cogitosus's *Life of St. Bridget* of the mid-seventh century, the *Táin Bó Fraích* of the eighth or ninth century, Irish sources for St. Bridget of the ninth century, and the twelfth-century *Life of St. Kentigern*. Another striking early instance is this: the international wonder tale about the Ogre's external soul,[1] AT. 302, tells how a princess has been carried off by an ogre, and at a secret meeting with her the hero learns from her—information that she has herself extracted from the ogre—that the ogre's life is not in himself but hidden in some external object, and that if the object is destroyed the ogre will die. This is successfully done. The life is commonly inside an egg, which is itself hidden in some place difficult to discover; in one Scottish Gaelic version it is inside a trout inside an egg inside a duck inside a ram in a tree stump.[2] The tale is well known all the way from India to the British Isles; and the motif of the man who dies when his life in the external object is destroyed occurs in ancient Egyptian in the story of Anupu and Bitiu already referred to,[3] in the Sanskrit *Kathasaritsagara*,[4] in the Greek myth of Meleager, and elsewhere. Now, an Old Irish version of the story of The Death of Cú Raoi, belonging to the eighth or ninth century,[5] tells how Cú Raoi of Munster carried off Bláithíne from Ulster, how Cú Chulainn followed, had a clandestine meeting with Bláithíne and learned from her the secret that Cú Raoi had told her—that his life was in an apple which was in a salmon which visited a nearby spring once in seven years, and if he split the apple Cú Raoi would die. They waited seven years and the salmon was caught, and presumably Cú Chulainn split the apple, but the text is obscure here. There can be no doubt at all that this is a very early Irish version of a familiar international popular tale.

The Old Irish story of Conall Corc[6] tells how his uncle sends him to the King of the Picts with a secret message written on his shield in Ogam, ordering that he is to be put to death. He falls asleep on the journey, and a friend who can read Ogam notices this message and changes it to read that he is to be married to the King's daughter; and this is duly done. Here we have a special sub-version of a very ancient theme, the fatal letter, ST. K.978; a man is sent with a sealed letter which, unknown to him, contains orders for his execution. This is familiar to everyone in the story of David and Uriah in the Bible,[7] the ancient Greek myth of Bellerophon already known in the Iliad,[8] and elsewhere. But in this particular sub-version, which is ST. K.511, the letter is changed to read that the bearer is to marry the king's daughter, and this treatment is found not only in Old Irish but also in a number of Sanskrit stories and in a group of early Christian Egyptian documents of Greek origin,[9] and other sources. Besides that, it was used in two international popular tales, AT. 461, The Three Golden Hairs, and 930, The Rich Man and his Son-in-Law,[10] in which context it is known all over Europe and in large parts of Asia including China. The oldest sources for this especial treatment of the letter theme are Indian, and there is reason to believe that it is of Indian origin. The Irish story of Conall Corc goes back to about A.D. 700 in our oldest text, but as it happens it is not clearly expressed in this just what it is the Ogam message says, and this is not explicitly stated until a text which is probably a century or so later. In any case, here is a very striking theme, very old, very widespread, and probably hailing from India, which is found in Ireland in the Old Irish period and had probably got there by the seventh century at latest.

A further good example which I should like to quote is the ninth- or tenth-century Irish story of how Cú Chulainn killed his son.[11] Cú Chulainn begot a son in a far country, and laid on the unborn child various *geasa,* including not to tell his name to anyone. He also left a ring for him, with instructions that when the child had grown big enough to wear it he was to come to seek his father. When the boy is seven years old he comes to Ulster, refuses to name himself, and overthrows the Ulster warriors, so that Cú Chulainn is forced to kill him. I suppose it is unnecessary for me to point out that this is the well-known tale of Sohrab and Rustem in the Persian *Shah Nameh* of about the year A.D. 1000. Rustem begets a child in a distant land, and leaves the woman an armlet for the child to wear if it is a son. When the boy Sohrab grows up he comes with an army to help his father, but by a combination of treachery and ill-luck the two meet without either knowing who the other is, and fight; Sohrab is mortally wounded, Rustem dis-covers the armlet, and realizes he has killed his son. The same story is found in the non-Homeric Cyclic poetry, told of Odysseus and Telegonus, his son by Circe; and, of course, in the well-known ninth-century fragment of Old High German heroic poetry, the *Hildebrandslied*. There are also medieval tellings of the same theme in Russian heroic ballads, in Norse and Icelandic saga, and in western European romances.[12] As a folktale it seems never to have had very much popularity.[13] It is remark-able that the motif of the ring or armlet puts the Irish version in especially close relationship to the Persian. The late T. P. Cross believed it got to Ireland through Anglo-Saxon intermediaries.[14]

I shall begin the discussion of the international tale in early Welsh with the story which most obviously springs to mind, probably the oldest of the Mabinogion, *Cul-hwch and Olwen*.[15] It is generally recognized that this is an international tale, and Celtic scholars sometimes refer to it as How the Hero Won the Giant's Daughter. But it is necessary to be a little more precise here, for there are various international tales about heroes winning giants' daughters. The essential plot of *Culhwch and Olwen* is this: The hero wants to marry the ogre's daughter, whose quest has been fatal to many previous wooers, and he gets the help of a number of extraordinary men with strange qualities. They go to the ogre's house and meet the girl in secret, and she connives at the quest. They then demand her of the ogre, who sets a number of impossible tasks to be performed as a condition of his consent; but they are successfully performed by the aid of the wonderful helpers. This done, they kill the giant and the couple are married. There is, of course, a very large amount of extraneous material which has become adopted into this; for instance, the hunt of Twrch Trwyth which is really a quite separate story; and the whole thing has attached itself to the native legend of King Arthur; but what I have just described is the essential skeleton.

Now this is a very well-known international popular story, known to folklorists as Six go through the World, number 513A in the Aarne and Thompson catalogue.[16] The summary is that a hero wants to marry the daughter of a king or ogre, who is to be had by anyone who can perform the tasks her father sets, but those who fail are put to death. The hero gathers in his company a number of wonderful men with magic skills, and by means of these skills they succeed in performing the tasks, and the hero wins the girl. The story has a very common variant, number 513B, in which the girl's father demands at the start a ship which will sail on land and sea alike, which is provided by an old man to whom the hero has been kind; the rest of the tale is as in 513A. Both 513A and 513B are familiar all over Europe, but 513A is known in Asia as well, and the distinctive motif, the wonderful helpers, is believed to have originated in India since it is found in early Buddhist sources and modern oral tales from India and Western Asia, as well as China, Indo-nesia, Africa, and America.

It is, of course, well known that the oldest European version forms part of the Greek myth of the Argonauts, which is a combination of A T. 513B with A T. 313, The Magic Flight—a combination of the kind which, as I have already explained, is of rather frequent occurrence in folktale telling. The fusion of the two tales has re-sulted in the necessary modification of both, as often happens, including the loss of the beginning of The Magic Flight, for which 513B is substituted. The hero, Jason, is set the task of getting a magic object, the Golden Fleece, from a king. Here the quest of a magic object has displaced the wooing of the king's daughter, since the second half gives the daughter a different role. Jason has a wonderful ship, the Argo, and a band of wonderful or semi-divine helpers, the Argonauts. The king of Colchis sets him certain dangerous tasks to prevent his succeeding. At this point, A T. 313 takes over. The king's daughter, Medea, helps Jason perform the tasks by her magic, thus replacing the aid of the Helpers; and then they flee—in the Argo, however, not on a horse—throwing behind them objects which delay the pursuit of the father—in this case not a comb and the rest, but the hacked-up fragments of the body of Medea's brother.

Culhwch and Olwen keeps close to the plot of AT. 513A, but the Argonauts, an ancient Greek version of 513B, shows that the tale is very old indeed in Europe, so that there is nothing at all surprising about its turning up in Dark Age Wales; it is a story that might very well have got there under the influence of Imperial Rome in Britain. There is in fact one point about *Culhwch and Olwen* which suggests that its sources may actually have been related to some version of the conflation of 513 and 313 which lies behind the Argonaut tale, for though Olwen does not help in the actual performance of the tasks, as the heroine of AT. 313, and hence Medea, does, she does nevertheless collude with the hero about them and offer helpful advice. Now this is not part of AT. 513, in which the heroine is hostile at this stage, and it is worth suggesting that it is a trace of the same sort of fusion of 513 and 313 as was carried out very fully in the Argonauts.

In folk versions of AT. 513 the wonderful men gener-ally include a great runner who defeats the princess in a race; a skilful marksman who can shoot a fly's eye at a very great distance; a great eater; a great drinker; and a man whose hearing was so sharp that he could hear the grass growing. The extraordinary men who accompany Culhwch, and on whom the teller lavished such elabor-ate attention out of all proportion to the ordinary folktale, include these very men. They are Henwas the Winged—'no four-footed creature could ever keep up with him the length of one acre, much less any further than that'; Medr son of Medredydd, 'who from Celli Wig [in Cornwall] could shoot a wren at Esgeir Oerfel in Ireland'; Hir Erwm and Hir Atrwm, 'the day when they came to an inn they would raid three cantrefs to supply them, [and] they feasted till noon and caroused till night'; Sugn son of Sugnedydd, who would drink the sea dry; and Clust son of Clustfeinad who, 'though he were buried seven fathoms in the earth, would hear the ant fifty miles away when it set out in the morning from its lair'. These must be the original nucleus of Culhwch's Helpers, to whom dozens of others became added in time, including the prototypes of some of King Arthur's Knights. Inciden- tally, one of Culhwch's Helpers is Gwefl son of Gwas- tad, who, when he was sad, would hang his lower lip down to his navel and throw the upper one over his head like a hood. There is a very odd coincidence here with the stock description of negroes in Persian literature, such as one whose upper lip ascended above his nostrils and whose lower lip hung down on his collar; and in modern Greek folktales the black negro ogre regularly has an upper lip reaching towards the sky and a lower lip touching the earth.[17] I do not say that there *must* be a connexion here, as the motif is a very exiguous one and might well be polygenetic, but it does look very much as if the otherwise inexplicable Gwefl is a negro, and it is very possible that we are dealing with a stock description which is international and old.

Since I have begun with *Culhwch and Olwen,* and the tale is probably the oldest of the Mabinogion in its present form, I might as well continue with some of the other international motifs in it before starting on the *Four Branches.* When Culhwch and his men come to the house of Custennin the shepherd the latter's wife recog- nizes that Culhwch is her nephew. She rushes to em- brace him, but Cei snatches up a log and thrusts it between her open arms, and she squeezes it in a hearty embrace that reduces it to a twisted withy.[18] This motif is a common international one in the story The Oldest on the Farm, A T. 726;[19] a very ancient old man, apparently feeble and helpless, welcomes a visitor by offering to shake hands, but the visitor, previously warned, holds out to him an object such as an iron stick or plough-share which the old man reduces to a twisted mass in his hand, remarking that young people nowadays have a very feeble handshake.[20]

The episode of the Oldest Animals in *Culhwch*[21] tells how as one of the tasks set by the giant Arthur's men seek for Mabon son of Modron, and ask news of him from a blackbird which is so old that over the years it has worn a smith's anvil down to less than a nut by sharpen-ing its beak on it. It has no news, but sends them to a still older stag, which is so old that it remembers a rotten tree-stump when it was an oak sapling and subsequently grew to a huge oak, but it has no news. It sends them to an owl, which is so old that the wood in which it lives is the third wood that has grown there since it remembers. It has no news, but sends them to a still older bird, an eagle which is so old that by standing on a rock each evening it has worn it to less than a handsbreadth over the years, but it has no news. It sends them to a salmon, which *does* know where Mabon is—imprisoned in Gloucester, which it regularly visits with each flood tide. There are no less than three international popular motifs here. The first is the group of animals each older than the preceding, the age being judged by their remembering the growth of a very old tree at various stages, or the like. This is found in the fourth-century Indian *Jatakas* and in other Buddhist works and other early Eastern texts, where a dispute between the animals about their age is involved. It has long been recognized that this is the source of the Oldest Animals in *Culhwch*,[22] but the dispute has become changed there owing to the introduction of the second motif, as I shall point out in a moment. Professor Thomas Jones has shown[23] how the Oldest Animals—the Eagle, the Salmon, the Stag, the Blackbird, the Toad, and the Owl, each older than the preceding (or the Stag, Salmon, and Eagle alone)— exist in medieval Welsh story independently of the search for Mabon. The tale of an eagle seeking information from an old stag (which remembers a stump when it was a sapling), which cannot give it but sends the eagle to an old blackbird, which cannot give it but sends the eagle to an old, blind salmon, is found in Early Modern Irish in the story of the eagle Léithín.[24] The information in question is whether they remember a night colder than the one preceding the eagle's quest. Very much the same has been recorded as a folktale in Mayo[25] (and doubtless elsewhere in Ireland); a crow which is so old that in sharpening its beak on the sock of an anvil it has worn it as fine as a needle, goes to a still older eagle to ask if it remembers a worse night, and the eagle sends it to a still older blind trout. The story is known in Scotland too, for a folktale from Lochaber[26] tells how an eagle travelled to discover a creature older than itself, and was sent by an old wren to a still older blackbird which had made a hole in an anvil by cleaning its beak on it, which sent the eagle to a still older stag, which sent it to a still older trout, which had become blind in almost exactly the same way as the Irish salmon and trout. It is obvious that the Eastern motif of the Oldest Animals was modified in the British Isles into a new form which appears in strikingly similar guise in Wales, Ireland, and Scotland.[27]

The second international motif in the British versions of the Oldest Animals is the way in which a seeker for information is sent by one old personage to consult a still older, and by *him* to one older still.[28] This is found in various international wonder tales, but notably in The Man on the Quest for his Lost Wife, AT. 400, who in his search is sent on from one old woman to her older sister and by her to a third sister still older. This motif is not in the Eastern versions of the Oldest Animals, and its introduction into the Celtic ones has resulted in its suppressing the incident of the dispute as to who is the oldest, though this has left a trace in the Scottish folktale, in which the eagle seeks to find a creature older than itself. The third international motif I referred to in the Oldest Animals episode in *Culhwch and Olwen* is found in that story alone, where it is obviously a late accretion as it is not even in the other Welsh versions. This is the search for the prisoner; and it is significant that this too belongs to AT. 400. At an earlier stage in that tale the man asks news of his lost wife from a succession of animals, but none can help him till he meets an eagle or a whale, which arrives late and says it has just been at the castle where she is imprisoned.[29] The similarity to the story in *Culhwch* is much too close to be accidental, and it is pretty clear that the teller employed this as a means of introducing the motif of the Oldest Animals into the story of the performance of the tasks imposed on Cul-hwch. No doubt he took it from some version of The

Man on the Quest of his Lost Wife because the incident of the inquiries from a series of progressively older
personages, already fused with the Oldest Animals on
Celtic soil, reminded him of that tale; and this would
mean that the international wonder tale AT. 400 was
already familiar in Wales.

You will remember that the essential plot of *Culhwch
and Olwen* is the international popular tale of the Helpers,
AT. no. 513. In some versions of AT. 513 the hero is
helped not only by extraordinary men but also by grateful animals to whom he has been kind; and we duly find
a trace of this in *Culhwch*.[30] The giant, Olwen's father,
says (or must have said, in an earlier version; the passage is a little obscure)[31] that long ago he sowed 18
bushels of flax seed in a certain field; that they never came
up; and that they must all be gathered up again, to the
very last seed, in one single day, and sowed once more to
produce a linen veil for Olwen at the wedding. In the
sequel, one of Culhwch's Helpers rescues some ants from
a blazing anthill, and the grateful creatures fetch in all
the seeds but one—with the charming additional touch
that even the missing one was brought in safely before
nightfall, by an ant that was lame. Now this motif is an
old friend in international popular literature and folklore
—though the lame ant is a purely Welsh fancy. It does
not really belong to AT. 513, but rather to AT. 313,
The Magic Flight, and 554, The Grateful Animals, a
story which is known throughout Europe and in India
and other parts of Asia, and occurs already in the
fourteenth-century Persian *Tuti-Nameh*. It is also found
in AT. 425, The Search for the Lost Husband, or
Cupid and Psyche. In the version of Cupid and Psyche

in Apuleius's *Golden Ass*,[32] which dates from the second century A.D., Venus sets Psyche the task of sorting out a great mixed heap of various grains before evening, and the task is done for her by kindly ants. But versions still closer to the Welsh are found in Asia. We have already seen it, in my first lecture,[33] in the tale of Sringabhuja in the eleventh-century Sanskrit *Kathasaritsagara*, where the hero has to sow 100 three-bushel measures of seed and gather every seed in again, and it is done by ants. Even closer, in a modern Indian folktale[34] Indra has had some land ploughed and twelve measures of seed ploughed into it, and the hero has to gather it all in without omitting a single grain; it is done by grateful ants. So in another modern Indian tale,[35] a king has mustard seeds sowed all over a great plain and orders the hero to gather them in into one pile all in one day, or be killed; the hero's wife does it with the magic help of doves, not ants this time. Omitting a number of other Asiatic versions, including modern Chinese and Japanese ones,[36] and the modern European folk versions,[37] a seventeenth-century Italian telling very similar to Cupid and Psyche occurs in the *Pentamerone* of Basile,[38] and of course there are two well-known examples in Grimm's Fairy-Tales,[39] both of them versions of AT. 554. In one, a man is set the task of collecting ten sackfuls of seed scattered by a princess before sunrise next morning, and in the other it is a thousand scattered pearls that are to be gathered in by sunset; in both the task is done by grateful ants whose lives the hero has spared. It has been shown that the motif is ultimately of Indian origin,[40] and it is certainly striking that some of the Asiatic versions best explain the obscurities in the account of *Culhwch*. The tale is at least as old, in Europe, as the Roman period in the second century A.D., as the use of one form of it in Latin by Apuleius shows; so that once again the theory that some inter-national tales reached Britain under the conditions of the Roman Empire may well be plausible—though I do not mean to imply by this, of course, that the account in *Culhwch* has any connexion with Apuleius. It cannot have, since it is much nearer to the Asiatic examples than to Apuleius.

Coming now to the *Four Branches* of the Mabinogion, there are several important international themes in *Pwyll*, which I will discuss in the order of their appearance. First, you will remember that Pwyll makes a bargain with Arawn, a king of the Otherworld, whereby in a year's time Pwyll is to fight a duel on Arawn's behalf with Hafgan, another king of the Otherworld, and that Pwyll is to be transformed by magic now into Arawn's own form so that no one knows it is not Arawn him-self.[41] This, as Arawn explicitly says, will involve Pwyll in sleeping with Arawn's wife in Arawn's shape. Mean-while, Arawn will take Pwyll's place in his guise in his kingdom. The exchange is made; but the first night when Pwyll and Arawn's wife go to bed Pwyll makes no approach to her, to her surprise, and so he continues throughout the period of the specified year. Once the duel is over the two men exchange shapes again, Arawn returns to his wife, and is astonished and delighted to discover Pwyll's loyalty. Now, this is a familiar theme among international popular tales, and is known as The Chaste Brother or The Chaste Friend.[42] It generally forms part of the story of The Two Brothers with the life-tokens which I summarized in my first lecture, mention-

ing the motif then. When the younger twin brother goes
to seek his lost elder brother he comes to the latter's home
and, being exactly like him, is taken by everyone for
him, including his wife. It is necessary that the younger
brother shall pass himself off for the elder, and consequently he has to sleep with his sister-in-law; nevertheless, he remains chaste, laying a naked sword in the
bed between them as a symbolical barrier and token of
chastity. Forming part of the story of The Two Brothers,
this motif has, of course, shared the immense popularity
of that tale as a whole; but it is also found used separately
in other tales, such as in Aladdin in the Arabian Nights,
and it occurs for instance in the Talmud.[43]

It is certain that the Welsh story-teller must have
known this motif in some form, and employed it in the
tale of *Pwyll*. But more than that; there is very good
reason to think that the whole episode of the exchange
of shapes, the Chaste Friend, and the duel come from
international sources. It was pointed out in 1944 by
Bar[44] that the Old French *chanson de geste* of Amis and
Amile contains these same features. These two friends
are exactly alike in looks, and in one episode Amis takes
the place of Amile in an ordeal by combat against his
enemy Hardré while Amile acts the part of Amis in
Amis' own home, but respects his wife's chastity, laying
a naked sword between them in bed. The *chanson* itself
is not earlier than the end of the twelfth century, but the
story is already told in a Latin poem composed by Raoul
le Tourtier between 1090 and 1100. The similarity to the
situation of the exchange of shapes, the Chaste Friend,
and the duel between Pwyll and Hafgan is so very close,
even allowing for the fact that the chaste friend fights the

duel in the one tale and the other friend in the other, that
an accidental coincidence is quite ruled out. Bar himself saw this, and thought it meant that the compiler of
the Mabinogion knew the Welsh translation of *Amis et
Amile*.[45] But this translation is doubtless scarcely earlier
than the Red Book of Hergest in which it occurs, so
this is impossible, and in any event the tale of *Pwyll* is of
course almost certainly at least as old as the time of Raoul
le Tourtier himself in its present, final, form and was unquestionably using much older sources. It is very extraordinary how scholars in other fields who touch on
Welsh literature in their researches seem so often quite
unaware that the *Four Branches* and *Culhwch* are very
early tales even as we now have them. The episode of
the exchange of shapes, the Chaste Friend, and the duel
must therefore have existed, *already* joined together, as a
current popular tale before the latter part of the eleventh
century, and this was used independently in France and
in Wales. The story of Pwyll demanded that he should
go to the Otherworld and fight Arawn's enemy on
Arawn's behalf. At some stage in the history of the
growth of *Pwyll* some teller who knew a version of this
popular conflate exchange-and Chaste-Friend-and-duel
motif saw how well this could be used in the Welsh tale,
and adopted it accordingly. It is scarcely probable that
the third alternative—namely, that the episode reached
France from Wales through Norman-Welsh intermediaries—can be correct, for chronological reasons,
though it is perhaps not impossible. The identical
appearance of the two friends is certainly better motivated
in the Welsh, and the Frenchman, rejecting the magic
and enchantment, would have been forced to fall back

on a fortuitous similarity of appearance. But this still does not prove that the French version comes from the Welsh. The point is in any case of more interest to French than to Celtic scholars; so far as present purposes go, *Pwyll* unquestionably contains a motif of widespread international character, the Chaste Friend, and the combination of this with certain other motifs appears also to derive from international sources.[46]

It is remarkable that this part of the story of Arawn and Pwyll contains still another very familiar international theme. Arawn warns Pwyll beforehand that in the coming duel he is to give Hafgan one single blow only and no more, however much Hafgan begs him to repeat it, because if he gives another Hafgan will be as well as ever again.[47] Now Gruffydd regards this as a device on Arawn's part to make Pwyll believe he has killed Hafgan when really he has not, because according to Gruffydd's theory the whole fight is really a sham.[48] But what Gruffydd apparently did not know is that we have here an international motif which is found in folklore from Arabia, Turkey, Egypt, the Caucasus, Russia, and Lapland in the east to Ireland and Iceland in the west, being especially common in the Near East and in eastern Europe, and occurring in literature in the Arabian Nights tale of Saif al-Muluk and in the Middle English poem of 'The Turke and Gawain'.[49] The theme is that when a hero fights a supernatural being he is warned beforehand—or sometimes at the very moment—that he must strike it only once, which will cause its death, but if he strikes it again it will come to life as good as ever. Thus in an Irish folktale from Corcaguiney, a man is attacked by a *sprid*, a spook, and thrusts his bayonet into it. The *sprid* asks for another thrust, but the man's companion advises him against it, and the *sprid* collapses in a mass of slime. In an Egyptian Arab tale, a hero attacks the son of the Sultan of the Jinns, who is in the form of a bull, and strikes it with his dagger; the bull asks for another stroke, but the hero has been warned, refuses it, and it dies. It is evident that the Welsh story-teller knew this widespread folk motif, and that is why it appears in his tale, since Hafgan was a king of the Otherworld and therefore a supernatural. His audience would no doubt be familiar with it too and would perfectly well understand why it is used here. There is, therefore, nothing in this incident in *Pwyll* to support the odd idea that the duel between Hafgan and Pwyll was really to be a bogus one.

Further on in the story of Pwyll we have the episode where Rhiannon gives Pwyll advice which results in his entrapping his enemy Gwawl inside a magic bag, which is hastily tied tightly once he is there. Then Pwyll summons his men, and they kick and thrash the bag, pre- tending that they are baiting a badger tied up inside, until at last they are persuaded to let Gwawl go.[50] This can scarcely be independent of a motif[51] which is attached in many versions to the international popular tale known as The Smith Outwits the Devil,[52] best known in Britain in the legend of St. Dunstan. This part of the story tells that the hero, who is being sought by Death or the Devil so as to carry him away, outwits him by deceiving him into going inside a magic haversack which he has, out of which it is impossible to escape until he allows it; and once he is inside, the hero has the sack pounded by black- smiths on an anvil, or so pounds it himself, until the one inside begs to be let go and promises never to trouble him again. The story is known as a folktale practically throughout the whole of Europe. I may quote a Scottish Gaelic instance:[53] An old soldier meets the Devil and flatters him into getting inside his haversack, which he then takes to a barn and has twelve men thrash it there with flails for two hours, and afterwards to a smithy where twelve smiths hammer it. Lastly, he takes it to a furnace and is about to throw it in when the Devil begs to be let go, promising him he shall never see him again. In the Welsh tale this has been combined with the motif of the request for enough food, &c., to fill a comparatively small vessel, which, however, turns out to be impossible to fill;[54] one of the group of international motifs about impossible tasks.[55]

The story of the stealing away of Rhiannon's child has been discussed a number of times, but I think it is still not fully explained. The tale is[56] that Rhiannon bears a child and six nurses are set to watch them at night, but the nurses fall asleep and when they wake the boy has vanished. There is a bitch with new-born puppies in the room, and the terrified nurses kill some of the puppies and smear the blood on Rhiannon's face and hands, throw the bones before her, and swear that she herself killed the child. Rhiannon's denial is not believed and she is made to do a humiliating penance for a long time. The tale continues that there was a man in Gwent called Teyrnon whose mare used to foal every May-Day eve, and the foals always disappeared. This year Teyrnon watched by the mare that night, and when it foaled a great claw came through the window and attempted to steal the foal. But Teyrnon cut it off at the elbow with his sword, and, hearing a scream, rushed out in pursuit but could see nothing. On his return he found the foal and the claw, and a swaddled infant boy as well. He and his wife reared the boy, and he grew rapidly to a size and strength beyond his years,[57] and before he was five years old he got the grooms to allow him to water the horses (that is, he was fond of horses). Teyrnon had the horse which was foaled that night broken and given to him, 'because', his wife says, 'the night you found the boy the foal was born and you rescued it'. In the sequel the boy is recognized as Rhiannon's son and is named Pryderi.

It is obvious, as all agree, that this story as it stands is confused and senseless and must have undergone some considerable corruption. The fusion in it of two motifs has been clearly recognized by scholars,[58] but in my opinion there is a third motif which provides an essential clue and has not hitherto been so well understood. Of these three, one is perhaps international and the other two certainly are.

The first motif is a favourite international one, known as the Calumniated Wife.[59] Of this there are two chief forms. In one, K. 2115 in Thompson's *Motif-Index*, the children are stolen either by some mysterious agency undefined or by a jealous relative; puppies or other young animals are substituted; and the mother is accused of giving birth to monsters, with the implication of bestiality. The other, Thompson's K. 2116.1.1, has the children stolen in the same way, but young animals are killed and the bones scattered, and the mother is accused of killing her children; this has a sub-type, K. 2116.1.1.1, in which blood is smeared round her mouth and she is charged with eating them. These motifs are found in a number of popular international tales, such as AT. 451, The Twelve Raven Brothers; AT. 652, The Prince whose Wishes come True; and the group AT. 706 (The Maiden without Hands), 707 (The Three Golden Sons), 710 (Our Lady's Child), and 712 (Crescentia). Belong-ing as they do to so many and such popular tales, these motifs are very old and have a very wide range. I would mention the story of Padmavati in the Sanskrit *Mahavastu* of, perhaps, the sixth century A.D.[60] The wives of a king steal the twin infants of one of their number, Padmavati, of whom they are jealous, and throw them in the Ganges in a box; they daub her face with blood and accuse her of eating them. She is condemned to death, but saved, and the children are later recovered. It is obvious, of course, that this is the same as the episode in the story of Rhiannon, in which likewise the accusation was prob-ably 'eating', for though the Welsh says merely 'you have yourself destroyed your son' the smearing of the blood on her face implies that she was charged with actually eating him.

The second motif involved in this episode is best represented in a number of Irish stories, as Kittredge has shown in his notable study on the whole complex of tales, of which the Irish story *Feis Tighe Chonáin* is the oldest and best. The earliest complete text of *Feis Tighe Chonáin* which we have is in a seventeenth-century manuscript,[61] but the story is doubtless older. In chapters 11 to 16 it tells how a giant used to come to the house of a certain woman and steal her children as soon as they were born, by sticking his arm through the smoke-hole in the roof. The Hero Finn mac Cumhaill with eleven magic helpers is set to watch next time the woman bears a child; and there is present in the room at the same time a pregnant bitch (really a woman thus enchanted by a jealous rival) which bears twin puppies at the same time as the woman bears the child. That night when the giant sticks his arm through the smoke-hole the Strong Helper tears it off, but the giant succeeds in escaping with the child. Finn and the Helpers track the giant to the top of a sea cliff, where they find him asleep, with six children and two puppies. They steal all these and flee in a boat, and the giant is killed as he pursues them. The children are those who have previously been carried off from the woman; and the puppies are obviously those born that night by the were-bitch, though this is not expressly stated in the seventeenth-century manuscript of *Feis Tighe Chonáin*, but it is stated in other copies.[62] Finn keeps the puppies, and they grow up and become his famous hounds Bran and Sceolang.

As Kittredge has clearly shown, the Helpers in this part of *Feis Tighe Chonáin* and in the complex of modern Irish and Scottish Gaelic folktales related to it are an extraneous feature. In fact they are simply the Six Wonderful Men whom we have already seen in the international tale AT. 513, who were so extraordinarily elaborated in *Culhwch and Olwen*;[63] or rather—which Kittredge did not realize—they are a special expression of this same motif seen in another international tale, AT. 653, in which the rescue of a princess stolen by a monster and kept on a sea-cliff is successfully performed by six Magic Helpers, and the pursuing monster is shot from the boat as they flee. Kittredge's account of the problem is not perfectly satisfactory, as he did not know a good and complete text of *Feis Tighe Chonáin* and did not fully realize its superior importance as compared with the modern folktales, but by and large his conclusions still hold good. He shows[64] that when the extraneous and secondary Helpers are removed the basic tale behind *Feis Tighe Chonáin* and the others is as follows: A king has two children who are carried off as soon as they are born and no one knows what has happened to them because the watchers are overcome by sleep. When the third child is to be born a hero is set to watch; he resists the sleepmaking magic and tears off the gigantic arm which comes down the smokehole to steal the child, but the monster escapes. According to Kittredge it leaves the child behind,[65] but in *Feis Tighe Chonáin* and almost all the other tales of the group he escaped with it,[66] and there can be no reasonable doubt that this is original. There is no need to enter here into the history of this tale in Ireland, beyond remarking that by an early fusion with a completely different story, Gelert the faithful hound, a new group of Irish tales arose from it,[67] in which the hound is substituted for the hero and bites off the gigantic arm; but this is entirely secondary and has no relevance to the tale in *Pwyll*.[68] The story behind *Feis Tighe Chonáin*, as just summarized, appears to me to be a fusion, probably arising on Celtic ground, of two international motifs which otherwise occur separately; one being the tale of the gigantic arm that reaches into a house with hostile intent and is cut or torn off by a hero, which is found already in the Sanskrit *Kathasaritsagara*[69] and in Beowulf among other sources,[70] and the other the motif of the witch who steals the newborn child, Stith Thompson no. G. 261.

The third motif which has been used in the episode in

Pwyll is an international one, whose presence there has
not been properly recognized hitherto. It is true that
Rhys hinted at it in 1886,[71] though he did not work out
how it affected the growth of the tale, and Kittredge also
considered it,[72] but he rejected it because he did not weigh
sufficiently carefully the sequel of the story of *Pwyll*.[73] I
refer to the motif known as 'congenital helpful animals',
no. B. 311 in Thompson's *Motif-Index*.[74] This generally
occurs as the introductory episode in AT. 303, The
Two Brothers, and is, therefore, very old and very widely
known. It goes as follows: a woman, a bitch, and a mare
all give birth at the same time (in The Two Brothers tale
they all have twins), and the animals are brought up with
the boy as his pets and later become his helpful com-
panions on his travels. It is often stated or implied that
these simultaneous births have a supernatural common
cause, which means that the animals are especially closely
linked to the boy, almost his brothers. Sometimes there
is only a dog, and sometimes only a horse, but generally
both occur. It is usually held that the very old Irish tale
of the Conception of Cú Chulainn contains a corrupt
version of this, and that in the uncorrupted original Cú
Chulainn was born at the same time as a mare foaled in
the house, and the twin foals were given him and grew
up to be his famous chariot horses, the Liath Macha and
the Dubh Sainghleann.[75]

Now, how are we to envisage the way in which the
present form of the episode in *Pwyll* was built up out of
these three motifs—the Calumniated Wife, the Monster
Hand and Child, and the Congenital Animals? I
suggest as follows. We begin with the story of The Hand
and Child, in its older form before the interpolation of

the Helpers. In this hypothetical original Welsh basis, Rhiannon's children, and the puppies of her dog, were mysteriously stolen away the night they were born, the nurses having fallen asleep. A hero (who appears in the final form as Teyrnon) is set to watch when another child is born and succeeds in resisting the soporific magic; a gigantic arm comes down the smoke-hole and he cuts it off, but the monster escapes with the child and puppies. The hero pursues and recovers them, and when the child grows up the puppies become his favourite dogs. This analysis, you will observe, is very close indeed to the story in *Feis Tighe Chonáin* and the other Gaelic versions of the Hand and Child, minus the Helpers. In *Feis Tighe Chonáin* the puppies become *Finn*'s hounds, but the fact they were born at the same time as the child strongly suggests they were originally the child's congenital animals, and I think they were transferred secondarily to Finn because of the great fame of his hounds Bran and Sceolang.[76]

This original tale was, I suggest, badly broken up and altered by the later introduction of the other two motifs. There is some reason to believe that Rhiannon was in some way associated with horses, if not originally actually a horse goddess.[77] This fact, together with the motif of the congenital dogs already in our tale, gave some story-teller the idea of introducing the well-known motif of the congenital horse which is generally associated with the congenital dog in the international tale AT. 303, which he must have known. Hence he made a mare foal in the house at the same time, and had the monster steal this foal along with the other two young creatures; the hero, however, having cut off the arm, ran after the monster and rescued all three. In the sequel the child grew up to be very fond of horses (and presumably of dogs too, but all trace of this is lost), and the congenital foal was presented to him as his very own, exactly as in the original tale of the Conception of Cú Chulainn (as Rhys already noted), 'because the night you found the boy the foal was born and you rescued it'. This alone will account for the otherwise unexplained episode in *Pwyll* of the young boy and his fondness for horses, and the present of the congenital horse to him.

Then came the third stage in the disintegration of the tale. Another teller, noting the mysterious abstraction of the children, and also the presence of the bitch with its new-born puppies in the room, was moved by these similarities to interpolate an entirely unconnected motif, the well-known international theme of the Calumniated Wife in its form K. 2116.1.1.1, the woman charged with eating her child. The watchers who had previously fallen asleep under the influence of the monster's magic are now replaced by the careless and drowsy nurses, who make use of the new-born puppies to kill some of them and forge the accusation of child-eating which is brought against Rhiannon; whence her condemnation to seven years of penance.

It was the clumsy patching at this stage of the tale, con-sequent on the violent introduction of the Calumniated Wife, which has left it practically unintelligible in its present form. Who stole the child? What was this mysterious claw? Why did it steal Teyrnon's foals? How did it come to drop the child in Teyrnon's stable and what was it doing there anyway? These are some of the questions which arise when we first read *Pwyll*, and the tale provides no answers—the answers are only to be found by the methods of comparative folktale study. In my view, what happened as a consequence of the inter- polation was this.[78] In the international Calumniated Wife the children are stolen by some mysterious agency never clearly defined, or more usually by jealous relatives or the like, but not by a monstrous claw. The monstrous claw consequently disappeared from this part of the tale, and with it the hero who was set to watch for it. At the same time, however, the claw is a very striking and dramatic theme, and the teller did not entirely forget it; he felt in a muddled sort of way that it had to be included, so he tried to transfer it to another part of the story and a later stage. It was necessary that it should be later, and not the same night, with the child recovered the next day as in the Hand and Child tale, because there had to be time allowed for Rhiannon's penance before the finding of the child, which, the previous loss of other children having been suppressed, had as yet had no opportunity of appearing. In the original Hand and Child the mon- ster goes directly to his dwelling on the cliff, and it is ridiculous that he should be carrying the child around with him when he steals the foal nearly 100 miles away some considerable time later. In fact this is clear evidence that at an early stage the two stealings must have been simultaneous, as I have already said. The result is that Teyrnon has been transferred from being the watcher in Rhiannon's room to a distant part of Wales where he is the person whose foals are stolen every May-Day eve. A further consequence of the interpolation is that the character of the puppies as future helpful animals ceased to have any significance and vanished altogether, since their presence in the room now played a completely different part; that is to say, to supply blood and small bones like those of an infant. At the same time the congenital horse was transferred, with Teyrnon and the claw, to the subsequent stage; indeed it was plainly no longer understood, and its congenital helpful character has become unclear and vestigial, in the form of the boy's fondness for horses and the present from his foster-parents. Neither horse nor dog plays any significant part in the sequel—all this has been lost. The watching hero, moved from Rhiannon's room to his own stable in Gwent, still pursues the claw, but not to the monster's cliff home to recover the stolen young creatures; all this has vanished along with the vanishing of any clear idea about the monster claw stealing Rhiannon's child, and the boy and foal are dropped at Teyrnon's house instead. He could no longer pursue and recover the child, for no child was now stolen from him; instead, the child is left in his stable and with it the foal.

If the above reconstruction is carefully examined I think it will be found to make sense. It agrees very largely with Kittredge, whose detailed arguments can be consulted by anyone who cares to do so; but it differs from him in some respects, particularly in the matter of the congenital animals, which I think he misunderstood. The whole tale in this branch of the Mabinogion is very confused, but the clue is to be found, I believe, along the lines laid down by Kittredge.[79]

[1] See BP. iii, 434.

[2] J. G. MacKay, MWHT. i, no. 1, p. 22. The egg–duck–sheep hiding-place is common in Scotland and Ireland.

[3] Masp., pp. 14 ff.

[4] Tawney, ii, 85.

[5] See R. I. Best, *Ériu*, ii, 18 and 32 ff.; Thurneysen, IHK., pp. 432 ff.

[6] See V. Hull, *Publications of the Modern Language Association of America*, lvi (1941), 937 ff., and lxii (1947), 887 ff.

[7] 2 Sam. xi.

[8] vi, 155 ff.

[9] See J. Schick, *Corpus Hamleticum* (i, Berlin, 1912; ii–v, Leipzig, 1932–8); M. Schlauch, JCS. i, 152 ff.

[10] See Aarne, FFC., no. 23, pp. 69 ff., and Tille, *Zeitschrift des Vereins für Volkskunde*, xxix (1919), 22 ff.

[11] See Thurneysen, op. cit., pp. 404 ff.; and T. P. Cross, JCS. i (1950), 176 ff.

[12] See M. A. Potter, *Sohrab and Rustem* (London, 1902); Köhler, KS. ii, 256 ff.; J. de Vries, *Ogam*, ix, 122 ff.

[13] It is ST. N. 731.2.

[14] Op. cit., pp. 181 f.

[15] M., pp. 95 ff.

[16] See BP. ii, 79 ff.

[17] See W. R. Halliday, *Indo-European Folktales and Greek Legend* (Cambridge, 1933), p. 37.

[18] M., p. 110.

[19] See R. Christiansen, *The Migratory Legends* (FFC., no. 175), pp. 86 ff., no. 5010.

[20] Cf. TGSI. xxv, 140 f.; and the tale about the Glaistig of Lianachan, J. G. Campbell, SHS., pp. 168 ff. (the motif of her twisting the plough-share, &c., appears more clearly in an unpublished version in the School of Scottish Studies).

[21] M., pp. 124 ff.

[22] See E. B. Cowell, *Y Cymmrodor*, v, 169 ff.; W. J. Gruffydd, *Y Cymmrodor*, xlii, 129 ff.; Eleanor Hull, *Folklore*, xliii (1932), 376 ff.

[23] *Journal of the National Library of Wales*, vii (1951–2), 62 ff.

[24] See Hyde, *Celtic Review*, x, 166 ff.

[25] Ibid., pp. 212 ff.

[26] *An Gàidheal*, iv (1873), 285.

[27] The Scottish version from Lochaber is very likely the most primitive, since the point of the quest there, to find an older animal, is closer to the Oriental story than any of the others are.

²⁸ See list of references in the *Journal of American Folklore*, xxx (1917), 380 n.

²⁹ Cf. VF., p. 157.

³⁰ M., pp. 114 and 127.

³¹ The account given here represents partly what he appears actually to say and partly what the sequel shows he must have said, in some more original form of the tale.

³² Apuleius, *Metamorphoses*, vi, 10.

³³ See p. 12 f.

³⁴ See W. A. Clouston, *Popular Tales and Fictions* (London, 1887), p. 239.

³⁵ M. Stokes, *Indian Fairy Tales* (London, 1880), p. 142.

³⁶ See E. Cosquin, *Romania*, x, 140 ff.; M. Stokes, op. cit., no. 20; Clouston, op. cit., p. 236; W. Eberhard, CFT., nos. 1 and 7 (the second a version of AT. 313).

³⁷ See, for example, Clouston, op. cit., pp. 236 ff.; BP. i, 134 and ii, 19.

³⁸ v, 4.

³⁹ *Kinder und Hausmärchen*, nos. 17 and 62.

⁴⁰ E. Cosquin, *Romania*, x, 140 ff.

⁴¹ M., pp. 4 ff.

⁴² See ST. K. 1311.1 and T. 351; also BP. i, 554; and B. Heller in *Romania*, xxxvi, 36 ff.

⁴³ Cf. Heller, op. cit., p. 46.

⁴⁴ F. Bar, 'Le Mabinogi de Pwyll, Prince de Dyvet, et la Légende d'Amis et Amile', *Romania*, lxviii (1944), 168 ff. The parallel he quotes from the *Kathasaritsagara* is not a very good one.

⁴⁵ Edited by Dottin, RC. iv, 201 ff.; and by J. G. Evans, *Kymdeithas Amlyn ac Amic* (Llanbedrog, 1909). For the French *Amis et Amile* and its sources see MacEwen Leach, *Amis and Amiloun*, Early English Text Society, vol. 203 (London, 1937), introduction; and F. Bar, *Les Épîtres Latines de Raoul le Tourtier* (Paris, 1937).

⁴⁶ The complicated analysis of and attempt to explain the first part of *Pwyll*, including this episode, given by Gruffydd (Rh., chap. 2) is unacceptable; cf. p. 122 below. He appears to forget, and almost makes the reader forget, that Arawn did not in fact beget any child on Pwyll's wife— for one thing, Pwyll had not yet got a wife.

⁴⁷ M., p. 5.

⁴⁸ Rh., pp. 37 ff.

⁴⁹ The motif is ST. C. 742. See BP. iv, 395; Köhler, KS. i, 469 ff.; A. H. Krappe, *Revue d'ethnographie et des traditions populaires*, vi (1925), 432 ff.; Wesselski, MdM., p. 143. Irish examples, *Béaloideas*, ii, 61, 212; iii, 511.

⁵⁰ M., pp. 13 ff.

⁵¹ ST. D. 1412.1; or better 1413.9.1.

⁵² AT. 330, specially 330B; see BP. ii, 149, 157, 163.

⁵³ TWH., no. 42.

⁵¹ Examples, see MWHT. i, 350, 410.

[55] ST. H. 1010 ff.

[56] M., pp. 18 ff.

[57] This is, of course, a common feature in tales about heroes; see ST. T. 615.

[58] For a study on the tale see G. L. Kittredge, 'Arthur and Gorlagon', *Harvard Studies and Notes in Philology and Literature*, viii (Boston, 1903), 149 ff., especially 222 ff. and 240 ff.; A. H. Krappe, *Balor with the Evil Eye* (New York, 1927), pp. 80 ff.; and G. Murphy, *Duanaire Finn*, iii (Irish Texts Society, xliii; London, 1953), pp. xiv ff. and 177 ff.

[59] See M. Schlauch, *Chaucer's Constance and Accused Queens* (New York, 1927); A. Dickson, *Valentine and Orson* (New York, 1929), pp. 38 ff.

[60] See Dickson, op. cit., p. 39.

[61] Edited by M. Joynt (Dublin, Mediaeval and Modern Irish Series, vii; 1936).

[62] See Kittredge, op. cit., p. 275.

[63] See p. 74.

[64] Op. cit., p. 227.

[65] His text of *Feis Tighe Chondin*, which is very abbreviated, does not say which it did; hence Kittredge's mistake, which was probably suggested to him by the desire to make it fit the story in *Pwyll*.

[66] In fact only one version makes the giant leave the child behind.

[67] Gruffydd's statement that there is an abundance of examples of this tale in 'many other countries' apart from Ireland and Scotland (Rh., p. 59) is incorrect; the tale is exclusively Gaelic apart from its offshoot 'Arthur and Gorlagon'.

[68] See on this n. 79 below.

[69] See Tawney, i, 138.

[70] See further Kittredge, op. cit., p. 227. I am not in the least convinced by Von Sydow's attempt to make Beowulf derive from our tale (see Murphy, op. cit., pp. 184 ff.).

[71] *Hibbert Lectures*, pp. 501-3.

[72] Op. cit., p. 244.

[73] He rejected it partly because he noted that there were *already* congenital animals present, the puppies; but he failed to realize that the international congenital animals motif generally includes *both* a puppy *and* a foal.

[74] Cf. BP. i, 534 ff.; KS. i, 179 ff.; E. S. Hartland, *The Legend of Perseus* (London, 1894), iii, 191 ff.

[75] See Thurneysen, IHK., pp. 268 ff.

[76] In *Feis Tighe Chondin* itself the bitch is really a woman under enchantment, but this is foreign to all the other versions and must have entered it under the influence of the secondary development in which the story is fused with Gelert, the 'Arthur and Gorlagon' story; see above.

[77] Cf. Rh., pp. 103 ff., though I cannot accept by any means all Gruffydd's arguments.

[78] The previous stealing by the monster of the other children, which is a necessary part of the original Hand and Child tale, had probably already

dropped out at an early stage because in its application to the story of Rhiannon only *one* child was necessary, Pryderi himself.

[79] W. J. Gruffydd had read Kittredge, but apparently without very close attention (see Rh. 58 ff.). The version of the Hand and Child story which he adopts to explain *Pwyll* is not the one used by Kittredge (though Gruffydd neither mentions nor justifies this fact), but is the secondary offshoot into which the Gelert motif is fused, as in 'Arthur and Gorlagon'. Moreover, in contrast to Kittredge (but again without note or justification) he treats the Calumniated Wife as the basis and the other as having been inserted into it, instead of vice versa. Again, the version of this theme which he silently assumes to be the one in *Pwyll* is K. 2115, the accusation of bestiality (because it suits certain of his theories), whereas it is in fact quite clearly K. 2116.1.1 or 2116.1.1.1, the accusation of killing or eating. He says himself that the result has been the loss of all features of the Gelert tale except the presence of the dog in the room (which dog he believes originally bit off the claw in *Pwyll* as it did in 'Arthur and Gorlagon', for which there is no evidence whatever in *Pwyll*), and speaks on p. 59 of the 'otherwise inexplicable fact that a stag-hound was on guard in the chamber where the child slept'. But the presence of the bitch in the room is an essential part both of the Calumniated Wife (to provide puppies to kill) and of the non-Gelert, *Feis Tighe Chonáin*, type of Hand and Child (where the puppies are congenital); and therefore it needs no other explanation. Besides that, it was *not* a valiant guardian stag-hound in *Pwyll*, as Gruffydd implies, but a newly delivered and therefore weakly mother stag-hound bitch incapable of guarding the child; and in fact it was *not* on guard at all. Gruffydd seems to have been careless here. He appears to ignore the fact that Kittredge has proved that the tearing off of the arm by a guardian hero is original, and the presence of the watchful dog in 'Arthur and Gorlagon' very secondary. His attempt to treat the foal as a substitute for the stolen child involves physical absurdities such as making the nurses substitute a foal for the child in Rhiannon's bed and accuse her of giving birth to a foal, an animal as large as herself (p. 65). His reconstruction on p. 65 is wholly unacceptable.

IV

The International Popular Tale in Early Wales: 2

THE story of *Branwen*, coming next to *Pwyll* in the Mabinogion, though exceedingly interest, ing in itself, has little of interest to offer the student of the non-Celtic international tale. Instead, most of those episodes in it to which parallels exist outside Wales find their counterparts in Ireland. It has long been recognized that *Branwen* is the most Irish of the Mabinogion, if one may so express it; a passage like that at the end explaining the origin of the five provinces of Ireland has no meaning unless we relate it to the known history and traditions of Ireland, and Dr. Mac Cana has recently discussed a considerable number of other Irish parallels with conspicuous success and good judgement. Nevertheless, there are two or three themes in *Branwen* for which an international origin outside the Celtic area may reasonably be suggested.

Quite early in the tale we have the motif of the Iron House, which tells how enemies wish to get rid of a party of people by treachery, and how they invite them to a feast in a house or room made of concealed iron plates, and, having made them drunk, set fire to the wooden parts of the house, or to faggots piled round it, so that those in, side are in danger of roasting; though in the sequel they escape. In *Branwen* this tale is told of a giant and his wife and children and is set in Ireland.[1] There are, of course, familiar examples of this motif in early Irish story, telling, as Dr. Mac Cana has noted,[2] but I should like to draw attention to a European parallel which may suggest that its origin is continental rather than Irish. I have already referred several times to the motif of men with wonderful attributes, the Magic Helpers, which provides the key to the tales A.T. 513 and 653. Now in a good many versions of A.T. 513, one of the men is a person who can withstand any extreme of heat, or of heat and cold,[3] and is thus able, on behalf of the hero, to come safely through one of the tests or tasks set by the father of the heroine. The version in Grimm's tale no. 71, Six go through the World, includes a man who can alter the temperature of his surroundings by changing the angle at which he wears his hat. When the whole party comes to the king's house and has successfully accomplished the task of beating his daughter in a race, the king plots to get rid of them by feasting them in a room with an iron floor and doors, and by heating the floor underneath till it is red hot. The party are bolted in and cannot escape, but the Helper sets his hat straight and the room becomes freezing cold. The presence of the motif of the Iron House here is perfectly clear, though its application is different; and it is scarcely possible that it is wholly un-connected with the Iron House in early Welsh and Irish. Further research is needed on this, but a prima facie case seems to exist for the international origin of the tale in *Branwen* and in the Irish source.

Later on in *Branwen* we have the episode of the Irish-men in the Bags.[4] The Irish plot treachery against the Welsh company by making a large hall for them with 200 armed Irish warriors hidden in bags hung by pegs from the pillars of the hall. The intention is that the

Irish shall attack the Welsh when their unsuspecting party has sat down. But one of the Welsh, Efnisien, takes a look round beforehand, discovers the bags, and asks his Irish companion what they contain. The reply is 'flour'. Efnisien is suspicious, however, and, pretending to feel the flour, he squeezes the bags one by one with his hand, crushing the skull of the hidden Irishman each time. This motif of the treacherous concealment of armed men in sacks or other such containers with the intention of attacking an unsuspecting party of men is an international one,[5] and very old indeed. An ancient Egyptian tale[6] tells how an Egyptian general besieging a city sends hundreds of sacks into it, ostensibly containing presents, but there are really soldiers in the sacks who capture the city. The likeness to the story of the Trojan Horse is also obvious, but there is, of course, an even closer parallel to *Branwen* in the Arabian Nights. The Forty Thieves plan to destroy Ali Baba as follows: a pretended merchant drives 19 mules into the courtyard of Ali Baba's house for the night, each mule being laden with panniers consisting of two huge jars supposed to contain oil. One does so, but the other 37 have armed robbers in them. However, a clever servant girl discovers this and kills them all one by one, just like Efnisien, by pouring boiling oil into the jars. This tale is not confined to the Arabian Nights, but as a folktale it is international all over Europe, A.T. 954. There is little doubt that a version of the story that lies behind the Egyptian tale and A.T. 954 was known early in the British Isles, and that this accounts for the Welsh motif in *Branwen* and the Irish parallels noted by Dr. Mac Cana.

The Arabian Nights provides another striking like-

ness to an episode in *Branwen.* When the Welsh party
returns from Ireland they stay for 80 years in Gwales in a
palace which is a paradise of all delights, where they
forget all their past sorrows and all the sorrows in the
world. At last one of their number, more inquisitive
than the others, opens a certain door which they had
been expressly forbidden to open and thus breaks the
charm, and the paradise loses all its character.[7] It is
obvious that there is a general similarity to this in a motif[8]
found in several international popular tales,[9] namely the
prohibition on opening a certain door—Bluebeard is a
familiar instance. But the Arabian Nights provides an
application of this which is very much closer to the
episode in *Branwen,* so close that coincidence is surely
impossible, granting what we know of the history of the
international popular tale. In the Third Kalendar's Story
a man is carried off by a roc to a marvellous Oriental
paradise where, he says, 'such gladness possessed me that
I forgot the sorrows of the world one and all'. The lovely
women he finds there leave him alone with the keys to 40
rooms, telling him he may open 39 doors but not the 40th,
for if he does he must lose their company for ever. On
the 40th day he does open the 40th door, driven by curio-
sity, and at once a flying horse carries him away, and he
never sees the paradise again.[10] I do not believe that there
is no connexion here, all the more so since significant
parallels between the Mabinogion and the Arabian
Nights are not uncommon, as we have already seen; the
combination of the themes of the forbidden door and
the lost paradise is too extraordinary to be a coincidence.

The next tale in the Mabinogion, *Manawydan,* is very

poor in international themes, and those it does contain are trifling; it is perhaps significant that *Manawydan* is the least interesting and successful of them all. You will remember how Pryderi and Rhiannon in turn come to a magic castle and find in its courtyard a golden bowl on a slab, to which they stick by the hands and feet as soon as they touch them, and they cannot escape.[11] This is the international motif ST. D. 1413.7 or 1413.8, being a variety of a general group D. 1413 and following, which forms part of the international tale AT. 571, All Stick Together, popular all over Europe and known in the Near East. A fifteenth-century English ballad called 'The Tale of the Basyn' tells how an adulterer, the priest, the adulterous wife, her maid, the sacristan, and a carter are all made by magic to stick to a certain pot until the priest pays £100 for their freedom; and the same theme is found later in English ballads and chapbooks.[12]

Again in *Manawydan*, one of his fields of wheat is found to have been stripped bare of the ears on every stalk, one morning, and next morning the same has happened to the second field. So the third night Manawydan watches, and a great host of mice comes and breaks off the ears in the third field and makes off with them. Manawydan catches one of the mice, and it turns out that they are the soldiers and ladies of a wizard and had come in the form of magic mice to ruin Manawydan.[13] There is a remarkably close likeness to this in an English folktale recorded in 1825.[14] A farmer finds that the sheaves of wheat in his barn are tossed about every morning, so he watches, and a party of elves comes through the keyhole and begins to carry off the wheat straw by straw. He makes a rush at them and they flee, never to return. There is another very similar tale in the collections of the Irish Folklore Commission, from Cárna in Connemara, as Delargy has pointed out.[15] Two witches in the shape of beetles steal a man's wheat; they are caught and beg to be released, and take human form again. The tale is, however, not limited to Wales and Ireland, and hence has a good claim to be regarded as international.

When we come to the story of *Math* we are in the realm of unimpeachable international sources. I shall say nothing about the question whether this tale has anything to do with the myth of Perseus and Danae or other such international material, which has been discussed by W. J. Gruffydd,[16] as there is no space for me to treat of it here. Instead, I want to draw your attention to one minor motif and one major complex of motifs, both of them international. When Gwydion comes with his party to the court of Pryderi in the attempt to obtain Pryderi's pigs, he buys them from him with a present of twelve wonderful stallions and twelve wonderful greyhounds, richly equipped, and twelve golden shields; but these are not real, they are made by magic out of toadstools. The spell lasts for only one day, and next day they will all have become toadstools again.[17] Here, of course, we are on familiar international ground. It is a constant belief that money, gold, or other such presents given by the fairies or by the Devil, or by other supernatural creatures, deceive the recipient only for a short time, and that next day or after some similar short interval they will be found to have become dead leaves, dead fern, horse dung, or the like worthless object.[18] Another well-known Welsh instance is found in the eleventh-century *Life of St. Cadog*, where King Arthur demands of St. Cadog a payment of cows red in front and white behind, and Cadog, who finds it difficult to procure these, makes some to Arthur's specification by a miracle. But when Cei and Bedwyr come to fetch them they change into bundles of fern.[19] Here is a good example of a popular international folk-tale motif being used and modified by a monkish compiler of a saint's *Life*, as so often happened in medieval hagiography.

One of the most interesting passages in *Math* is the tale of how Blodeuedd and her lover Gronw plot to get rid of Blodeuedd's husband Lleu. They have to discover how Lleu may be killed, since it is apparently known by them that he cannot be killed in any ordinary way. Blodeuedd persuades him to tell her the secret, pretending to be anxious on his account, and he explains that the way to kill him is to make a spear which has been worked on for a year on Sundays only during Mass time; but that further, he cannot be killed inside a house nor outside a house, on horseback nor on foot. The only circumstances in which he can be killed are these: he must stand with one foot on the back of a he-goat and the other on the edge of a bath-tub with a thatched roof above it, and in that situation, if he is struck with the specified spear, he would be killed. Blodeuedd pretends to be satisfied with these very improbable circumstances, but a year later, when the spear has been made by Gronw, she has a tub of the kind described made and a he-goat brought, and gets Lleu to stand in the right position, ostensibly simply to illustrate to her what the situation is like in which he may be killed. Lleu is deluded into showing her, whereupon Gronw hurls the spear at him from his ambush. Lleu is not killed, however, but changes into an eagle and flies away.[20]

Some years ago this episode was interpreted as the myth of a god, in accordance with the theories of the folktale then fashionable in some quarters.[21] It was taken as part of the myth of a dying Corn God—Tammuz, Adonis, Attis, &c., and also the myth of a Sun God, apparently simultaneously, Lleu being identified with both gods at once. In point of fact it consists of two perfectly familiar international themes.

In the first place, the motif of the wife learning the secret of how her husband may be killed, and disclosing this to her lover, is, of course, an international one, ST. K. 2213.4.1,[22] and is closely related to the story of Samson and Delilah (K. 975). It appears already in the Egyptian tale of The Two Brothers belonging to the thirteenth century B.C., to which I have referred several times. There is a good example of it in the eighth- or ninth- century Irish tale of Cú Raoi, Bláithíne, and Cú Chulainn, which I mentioned in the third lecture. Cú Chulainn persuades Bláithíne to betray Cú Raoi, who had already told her where his life lay, namely in the golden apple in the salmon and the rest, as previously described; the story says he had told her this 'in his simplicity, to comfort her sorrow',[23] that is to say to calm her pretended anxiety on his behalf, just as Lleu thanks Blodeuedd for her *ymgeled*, her anxious care for him. In the story of Lleu, however, the motif does not lead to that of the external soul, the life hidden in some im- probable place difficult of access, but to a set of circum- stances which are never likely to come about in the ordinary course of events. It is this extraordinary set of circumstances to which we must now turn.

Lleu cannot be killed either in a house or out of a house, either on horse or on foot. The sequel, like so many sequels in the *Four Branches*, is not very clearly ex-plained, but it is nevertheless obvious even without external parallels that in standing on the edge of the tub, with its thatched roof overhead, he is partly in a house and partly out of it—or better, partly under a roof and partly not under it—and therefore neither wholly inside nor wholly outside. Further, having one foot on an animal and the other not, he is partly on an animal's back—though not indeed on horseback—and partly not, and therefore neither wholly on the back of an animal nor wholly on foot. If we knew no more than this the circumstances would still be a little puzzling in detail, though clear enough in their outlines. Fortunately, however, we do know more, for various expressions of this identical situation form part of an exceedingly popu-lar international tale, AT. 875, The Clever Peasant Girl.[24] Part of this story goes as follows: a certain king or chief sets a clever peasant girl a number of riddling tasks, which are on the face of them self-contradictory and absurd; however, the sharp-witted girl understands what is meant and performs them all to his satisfaction, and he is so pleased that he marries her. The tale then continues with further episodes which do not concern us. This story has been a great favourite; in his study on it de Vries mentions 262 versions from Ireland, Scotland, France, Portugal, the Basque country, Spain, Italy, Sicily, Germany, Flanders, Frisia, Denmark, Sweden, Norway, Russia, Poland, Czecho-Slovakia, Slovenia,

Croatia, Serbia, Roumania, Bulgaria, Greece, Lithu-
ania, Latvia, Finland, Hungary, Livonia, Lapland,
Turkestan, Mongolia, Arabia, Syria, Africa, and the
Philippines.[25] In addition to this, the same motif with the
same riddling tasks is found in a good many versions of a
quite different international tale, A.T. 921, The King
and the Peasant's Son, a story recorded in 295 examples
known to de Vries from much the same areas but including also Brittany, the Caucasus, and India ancient
and modern.[26] Further, it also occurs in some instances of
still a third tale, A.T. 920, The Sons of the King and the
Smith, which is practically limited to eastern Europe.[27]
De Vries knows the motif of the riddles in a total of 348
variants among these and other tales.[28]

The riddling tasks set vary in these many and widespread versions, but certain features are almost constant
and others are very common. Among the commonest are
these: the person set the tasks is to come to the person who
sets them neither naked nor clothed, neither on horse nor
on foot, neither indoors nor out of doors; less often,
neither washed nor unwashed. There are several other
such enigmas which may occur and which I need not
mention here, as they are not relevant to *Math*. It is usual
for any given version of these tales to list three of these
tasks, but there are sometimes more. The solutions are as
follows: neither naked nor clad, the person wears only
a fishing-net or a skin or other unusual clothing, or appears only half dressed. Neither on horse nor on foot, the
person comes riding on some other animal, most often
a goat (as in a Scottish Gaelic version given by Campbell of Islay)[29] or a donkey or a pig, and may have her
feet touching the ground as she does so; or she may rest

one foot on the back of an animal (again most often a goat or donkey) and walk with the other on the ground. A German tale has her come in a carriage drawn by a goat, standing with one foot on the goat's back and the other on the carriage; and a Sanskrit version of the four-teenth century has Rohaka, the hero, stand with one foot on a ram and the other on the hub of his chariot. Neither indoors nor out of doors, the heroine or hero stops on the threshold so that she or he is partly inside and partly out; this is the case, for instance, in the Scottish Gaelic story of Gráinne to which I have just referred.[30] Neither washed nor unwashed, the face or other part of the body alone is washed. The Sanskrit story of Rohaka makes him obliged to come neither by day nor by night, neither in the shade nor in the sun, neither in the air nor with feet on the ground, neither on nor off the road, and neither washed nor unwashed; and he comes at twilight, using a sieve as a parasol, with one foot on a ram and the other on the hub of his chariot, as just noted, driving along the gutter, and having washed only his neck. The oldest European version whose age de Vries realized is in the thirteenth- or fourteenth-century saga of Ragnar Lod-brok, in which Ragnar tells a beautiful girl called Kráka to come to him neither naked nor clad, neither fed nor fasting, neither alone nor accompanied by anyone; and she comes dressed in a fishing-net and her own long hair, chewing a plant, and accompanied by a dog.

Now I think you will agree, there cannot be the slight-est doubt that the episode in question in *Math* is a version of these riddles. Lleu specifically says that he cannot be killed in a house nor out of a house and neither on horse nor on foot; and I have already remarked that in the position where he stands he is partly under a roof and partly not, and is partly on an animal and partly not. As the story stands in *Math* one would have expected a horse, not a goat, but the international motif shows us perfectly clearly that the solution very often—indeed *most often*—is precisely a goat. As to his other foot, it is not on the ground, as in many versions, but is to be compared rather with Rohaka's foot on his chariot-hub, or with the German version in which the girl has one foot on a goat's back and the other on her carriage. Of course, a chariot or carriage will not suit in *Math*, where Lleu is not required to *come* anywhere but to stand still and be shot at. All the same, why have we got the tub here? Scarcely simply to supply the roof, because the motif concerning indoors and outdoors could have been arranged better with a mere hut, or a roof by itself, and a tub with a roof is unnatural. Surely the tub must refer to the motif of neither washed nor unwashed. Lleu does not specifically mention this as a condition, but in the story he does in fact bathe in the tub before standing on its edge and the goat's back, and it is surely obvious that the tale did originally include the condition 'neither washed nor unwashed', and that Lleu bathed only part of himself, not the whole. Finally, he stands in the specified position wearing only his trousers, and this must surely mean that he is neither naked nor clad, though once again this condition is not laid down in the story as we now have it.

De Vries was aware that this motif occurs in *Math*, but the really surprising thing is that he believed the Mabinogion is a collection of *modern* folktales—not to mention also the fact that he thought it is Irish.³¹ Moreover, he recognized in it only the two conditions which the story specifically mentions itself. The consequence is that he takes the thirteenth- to fourteenth-century saga of Ragnar Lodbrok to be the oldest European example, being unaware that *Math* is at least three centuries older; and hence his involved and lengthy theories about the history of the story are rather beside the point. This is a very striking illustration of the remark I made in a previous lecture—that many students of international popular literature, including some of the very best of them, pay scarcely any attention at all to the early Celtic literatures and display the most surprising unawareness of them, apparently quite without realizing that they are storehouses of popular tale material, both national and international, of the greatest richness.

Now, as I remarked just now, these motifs in *Math* are not applied to a problem set and to the demand that a person is to come to a certain place behaving in the manner described, as they are in all three of the international tales in which the theme usually occurs. Instead, these are the difficult conditions under which alone Lleu can be killed. It looks as if this is a very archaic feature, and that the application to the demand in question is a secondary thing, very widely developed in AT. 875, 920, and 921. In *Math*, we have rather the theme of magic invulnerability except in certain circumstances, again an international motif of which Achilles' heel is a well-known example. These themes are listed by Thompson under his Z. 311 and following. I may quote a parallel to *Math* which is striking because it is both so early and so similar. In the great Sanskrit epic the *Mahabharata*, which dates from about the time of the birth of Christ, there appears a demon called Vritra who is magically invulnerable. He can be killed neither by a dry thing nor a damp thing, neither by stone nor by wood, neither by shot nor by knife, and (a theme common to the story previously discussed, as in the tale of Rohaka) neither by day nor by night. In the sequel the god Indra stifles him at twilight with a lump of mud. The actual conditions are indeed different from those affecting Lleu, but the background is the same, and I suggest that possibly the neither-on-horse-nor-on-foot riddle and the rest may originally have been a condition of vulnerability of which traces remain in two very early sources.

The stories of the Mabinogion other than the *Four Branches* and *Culhwch* contain little of interest to anyone looking for international popular tales. There are, of course, a number of international motifs in them, but they are of a rather minor nature. I will mention briefly two or three of them before passing on to early Welsh literature outside the Mabinogion. At the beginning of *The Dream of Macsen* we have the well-known theme of the man who dreams of an unknown girl, falls in love with this dream girl, and has a search made till he finds her.[32] Here is an international motif, ST. T. 11.3, that has had considerable popularity,[33] particularly since it forms part of the international tale A.T. 516, Faithful John,[34] widely known in Europe and Asia. The motif occurs as early as the second century A.D. in Greek in Lucian's account of how Medea fell in love with Jason in a dream,[35] and it is familiar in Sanskrit literature and early Irish,[36] to mention only these. It is told in Scottish

Gaelic as the opening of the story about the sinking of the Spanish Armada galleon in Tobermory harbour.[37]

You will remember that in *Peredur* the hero sees a raven beside a newly killed duck in the snow, and compares the black raven, white snow, and red blood to the hair, flesh, and cheeks of the girl he loves.[38] This motif is, of course, known in early Irish, notably in the story of Deirdre, and also in modern Irish and Scottish Gaelic folktales,[39] but it is an international one for all that, ST. T. 11.6 and Z. 65.1. It forms part in versions of several international popular tales, such as AT. 709, Snow White,[40] AT. 510A, Cinderella, and others, and thus has a considerable distribution; I might mention the seven-teenth-century Italian example in the *Pentamerone* of Basile.[41] For a long time it has been the fashion to regard this motif as being of Irish *origin*,[42] and as having been spread in medieval romance through the influence of the French version, derived from the original of *Peredur*, in Chrétien de Troyes' *Conte del Graal*; and this goes back to Zimmer,[43] who pointed out that the version in the Deirdre story is the oldest known example of it. It may very well be that its appearance in other medieval rom-ances is due to Chrétien's use of the lost Welsh original of *Peredur*, but Zimmer did not realize that it is of wide-spread occurrence as a folktale motif as well. Besides, the history of the international popular tale was not well understood in his day, and he would not have con-ceived it possible that an international motif of continent-wide distribution could appear in Irish so early; hence the only explanation he could see was that since the oldest example is Irish it must be of Irish origin. But early Irish literature contains quite a number of familiar international themes certainly not originally Irish, as I have already pointed out, not to mention Welsh, and I see no good reason why this should not be another of them. It is found very early in Irish because early Irish literature is unusually rich and well preserved by comparison with all other vernacular European literatures.

Leaving the Mabinogion proper, the medieval Welsh story called *Hanes Taliesin*[44] tells how Gwion Bach is set by the witch Cyrridwen to watch and stir a boiling magic cauldron of knowledge, and three drops of the brew splash on his finger. When he sucks it he finds he has thus acquired the entire magic virtue of the concoction, making him a great sage and wizard. He flees the wrath of Cyrridwen and she pursues him; he changes himself to a hare to run the faster, but she turns herself into a grey-hound; he becomes a fish, but she an otter; he becomes a bird and she a hawk; he a grain in a pile of wheat, and she a hen who swallows the grain which was Gwion. She then changes back to human shape, and nine months later bears a child who becomes the poet Taliesin. Now the first part of this, how Gwion got his super-natural knowledge, is of course familiar in Irish as the story of how Finn mac Cumhaill got his magic 'thumb of knowledge' when he was set by a poet to cook for him a wonderful fish and, burning his fingers on it, sucked his thumb and found that he had acquired all the super-natural wisdom the poet should have had by eating the fish.[45] Nevertheless, it is an international motif, ST. B. 161.3, and forms the nucleus of the international tale AT. 673,[46] generally called The White Snake after Grimm's version of it. A well-known instance of the motif by itself is the Norse legend of Sigurd in the

Fafnismal in the Edda, in which Sigurd kills the dragon Fafnir and roasts its heart for his tutor Regin to eat, but burns his finger while prodding it to see if it is cooked, just like Finn, and having sucked it discovers he understands the language of birds; but the tale AT. 673 has a wider distribution than this.

The second part of the story of Gwion and Cyrridwen, the transformation flight, has given rise to a good deal of speculation about what has been claimed to be 'the Celtic doctrine of re-birth', and much ink has been spilt in the attempt to show that the Celts believed in the transmigration of souls into animals—which it can easily be shown they did not—and that our tale is a myth illustrating this belief in transmigration. In point of fact this episode in the *Hanes Taliesin* is a perfectly well-known international wonder-tale motif, the magic transformation flight, ST. D. 671, fused with another, the magic transformation contest between two wizards, D. 615, and this fusion is an episode in many versions of the very widespread international popular tale, AT. 325, The Magician and his Pupil, which I summarized in an earlier lecture, where I noted that it is popular in Europe and Asia and is probably of Indian origin. The magician's pupil is pursued by his master, just like Gwion and Cyrridwen, or by the other pupils, and changes himself into various creatures to escape, and the pursuers change themselves into appropriate creatures to catch him. What these creatures are varies somewhat in the many different versions, but they very commonly include a bird and a hawk, a fish and an otter, and sometimes a hare and a dog, and the whole ends with a grain of corn and a cock or other bird attempting to swallow it. These resemblances are much too close to be accidental, and this part of the *Hanes Taliesin* is simply a Welsh version of an episode in a familiar popular international tale. There is no need to look for doctrines of transmigration to explain it. The motif of a living being or other object being swallowed and born as a child is, of course, very well known in folk-belief and primitive story,[47] and this too has no connexion with 'doctrines' of rebirth but is an echo of a very early stage in human development when man did not yet know where babies came from.[48]

We might perhaps not think of Nennius' Latin *Historia Brittonum*,[49] compiled early in the ninth century, as a Welsh source for international popular tales; yet Sir Ifor Williams has pointed to a number of folktales in that extraordinary work,[50] and I should like to add remarks on a couple of international instances which he does not mention. An obvious case is the story of Carn Cabal in the section called the *Mirabilia*,[51] telling of the stone on the cairn in Breconshire bearing on it the footprint made by King Arthur's dog Cabal during the hunt of the boar Twrch Trwyth.[52] Footprints on rocks made by the Devil, the Saints, or other supernatural or wonderful beings are commonplace in the local legends of many parts of the world,[53] and it may very well be in this case that the origin is polygenetic, that is to say, that these tales (or some of them) are of quite independent origin, since such a belief is an obvious deduction from any hollow in a rock bearing a real or fancied resemblance to a footprint. What is certainly not polygenetic is another international tale in Nennius, the story of Cadell and his calf.[54] You will remember that St. Germanus and his party were driven inhospitably from his city gate by the wicked king Benlli, but Cadell, one of his servants, invited them to his own house. He had nothing on which to feed them but a calf; he killed and cooked it, and St. Germanus warned them all not to break any of the bones when they ate it. Next day the calf was found miraculously alive and whole along with its mother. We have here the international popular tale AT. 750B,[55] often called Thor's Goats after the Norse version in which Thor and Loki stay the night with a peasant who has no food for them, so Thor kills the goats which pull his own chariot, and they all eat them. Thor warns them to break no bones but to put them all on the goats' skins which are spread out, but the peasant's son breaks a bone to suck the marrow. Next day Thor collects all the bones and the goats arise alive again, except that one of them limps in one leg where the bone was broken. It is evident that in Nennius the tale is incomplete; St. Germanus' warning should have been disobeyed by some member of the household, with results similar to those in the story of Thor, but this has dropped out. This tale is widely known in Europe, and the instance in Nennius is the oldest recorded.[56]

This has brought us into the field of legends of the saints, which are often full of international popular motifs. To a considerable extent, of course, hagiography and other religious literature has its own popular learned motifs, stories of miracles and so on, repeated again and again from one *Life* to another and not appearing in ordinary folklore except where they are obviously derived from religious sources; the story of the dead dog and the stream of pure water quoted in an earlier lecture is an example of this latter process. By and large, however,

when a tale well-known in secular popular lore turns up
in a religious text I do not myself believe we are justified
in supposing, without strong supporting evidence, that it
is of religious origin and had spread from religious literature into popular lore, rather than vice versa, or not unless it has an essential religious point which cannot be
removed without destroying the tale. Thus it has been
claimed recently that the version of The Ring of Polycrates in the eighth- or ninth-century Irish hero-tale *Táin
Bó Fraích* was derived from an early version of the *Life
of St. Kentigern.* There are various reasons why I believe
this to be impossible,[57] including the fact that no version
of this *Life* is likely to have existed so early; but in general
The Ring of Polycrates is a motif that has been immensely popular in numerous variants from at least the
time of Herodotus; and though it is, of course, sometimes
used in religious contexts it is only in certain clearly
defined sub-types that it so appears. In all such cases, in
my own view, the probability is that a widespread
international popular motif has entered a hagiographic
context secondarily and not the reverse—like everyone else,
the monks knew the stories popularly current, and were
perfectly ready to use them. In particular the recent trend
in some quarters to derive much early Celtic secular literature, and especially heroic literature, from learned
Christian religious sources seems to me ill-judged and
likely to lead to unfortunate consequences.

Nevertheless, what one may properly call religious
folklore, both international and otherwise, is of enormous
interest, and it is strange that it has attracted comparatively little attention anywhere; yet early Celtic literature
is full of it. The mass of the more bizarre apocryphal

religious lore which grew up in the early Church, and especially the Eastern Church, seems to have had a very special attraction for the Celtic monks, and whereas this material largely disappeared from the religious literature of Europe at an early period it remained and flourished in the Celtic countries for centuries.[58] Hence a considerable number of apocryphal legends which occur in Irish, and to some extent Welsh, literature are otherwise known almost exclusively in eastern sources like Coptic and Syriac texts, as well as in continental European folklore and representations in medieval art, but very little in regular European religious literature. A proper study of this fascinating field, with a sort of Stith Thompson motif-index, is badly needed, and I have been urging it as a research project for many years. It would perhaps take a man who combined the qualifications of a Celticist like Sir Ifor Williams or Gerard Murphy with those of a medievalist and church historian like Montague James to do it really thoroughly, but any first-rate young Celtic scholar who was prepared to devote years to it could do a very worth-while job on it.

For instance, there is much in the Book of Taliesin which cannot be understood without a good knowledge of what I have called international religious folklore— the *Marwnat y Vil Veib* is an example, and another is the poem on the Judgement Day.[59] Again, we have the well-known Debate of the Soul and Body in the Black Book of Carmarthen, a favourite international theme, ST. E. 727.1.[60] A further good example is the story of the Miracle of the Instantaneous Harvest. This tells how on the flight into Egypt the Holy Family passed a field where a farmer was sowing seed, and the Virgin begged him to

tell Herod's men the truth, if they came that way, that
they had passed by when he was sowing his seed. By the
time Herod's men arrived the crop had miraculously
grown and ripened and was already being reaped, so the
pursuers turned back on hearing the farmer's answer,
since it was obvious to them that the party must have
passed there months before. This legend is widely known
in modern European folklore, in England, Scotland,
Ireland, Flanders, Holland, Sweden, France, Spain,
Portugal, Italy, Malta, Germany, Roumania, and Russia;
and also, outside Europe, in modern Aramaic, where it
is told of a Mohammedan holy woman fleeing an un-
welcome marriage. In medieval literature it is very much
rarer, though representations of it are sometimes seen in
medieval religious paintings. It is found in a fifteenth-
century French mystery play and some fifteenth-century
Flemish carols. Apart from these I know only two others,
both Celtic and both older than this. One is in an Irish
religious bardic poem of the thirteenth century attributed
to Donnchadh Mór Ó Dálaigh. The other, the oldest, is
in the Black Book of Carmarthen in the poem on the
miracles of God beginning on p. 41, which presumably
dates from the twelfth century. I need not discuss this
whole question in detail here, as I have already done so
elsewhere,[61] but the point is that this is a very fine example
of what one may call an international religious popular
tale. There is little doubt that its source must have been
some early Apocryphal Gospel text now lost, and that
its dissemination was in the first place through religious
written literature; that it appears in early religious sources
in Wales and Ireland because the Celtic Church was
particularly fond of apocryphal stories of the marvellous;

and that eventually it found its way into the folklore of the Near East and Europe. There is a rich harvest of material of this sort waiting to be reaped by a qualified scholar.

These lectures have dealt with the international popu-lar tale in early Wales, by which I mean stories and motifs shared by Wales with the European continent and Asia, and indeed sometimes with large parts of the world. I am thus precluded from discussing those other motifs in the Mabinogion and the rest which seem to be found only in Celtic sources (generally especially Irish) and may therefore be treated as an aspect of Celtic popular lore, not international. There are, of course, a good many of these. I might mention the first main episode in *Pwyll*, which is an example of the familiar Celtic theme that the fairies or inhabitants of the Other-world have wars and other contests between themselves in which the side which can enlist the help of a mortal will be victorious. Well-known early Irish examples are *Echtra Laegaire* and *Serglige Conculainn*. This fact was pointed out long ago by Baudiš,[62] though it is a pity that he was not aware of the valuable additional proof which exists in modern Irish folklore. Some authorities, impressed by the numerous Irish parallels to motifs in the Mabinogion —parallels which are mostly fuller and better repre-sented in Irish—have tended to regard these themes as of Irish *origin* and to hold that they spread thence to Wales, as part of a massive influence of Irish civilization upon early Wales. In the case of stories without parallels outside the Celtic countries this may very well be per-fectly true, and I would not for a moment attempt to deny it, though I think the extent of the unquestionable early Irish influence on Welsh literature and civilization has perhaps been a little over-rated by some scholars such as Vendryes. But in the course of these lectures a considerable number of international tales and motifs have been discussed which are found early both in Irish and in Welsh and yet are unquestionably not of Irish origin, some of them being certainly Eastern in background.[63] It could be argued, of course, that on their westward journey these reached Ireland first and then spread backwards to Wales, but this would surely be unnecessarily perverse. I have already suggested that some came to Wales—and why not thence to Ireland?—under the conditions of the Roman Empire; a distinguished American scholar has held that the Sohrab and Rustem story was brought to Ireland from Anglo-Saxon England.[64] International tales may have reached the early Celtic literatures in many ways, and indeed it is highly probable that some were current among the Celts on the Continent before the Roman Empire ever existed. In view of this, I would suggest that in discussing non-international tales found in the Celtic literatures it would be as well to suspend judgement and not to assume that they must be of Irish origin except in those cases, like the story of the five provinces of Ireland in *Branwen* and others, where there is some special very strong and peculiar evidence in support of this. Otherwise I think we should say: 'This story may have come from Ireland to Wales or it may have gone the other way.' I would suggest that we might envisage a sort of pool of popular themes known to all the insular Celtic peoples in early times, but now better preserved in Irish because

Irish has a much larger surviving early literature than any of the others.

In concluding these lectures, I should like to ask an important question about the early tales of the Mabinogion. How were they put together, and how are we to envisage them as having reached the final form in which we now know them? When I first began to study the elements which make up the Mabinogion, many years ago, I approached them on the assumption that they were written copies of actual tales taken down from the oral recitation of one of the early Welsh professional story-tellers, the *cyfarwyddiaid*. But more careful consideration of the evidence shows this can scarcely be possible. As we have seen, any good folktale teller of today can preserve without effort quite long and complex tales without ever losing his way or upsetting the logical sequence of plot whereby episode B follows necessarily upon and is explained by A, and C by B, and so on, and everything is accounted for and every thread neatly tied up at the end. If an ordinary folktale teller can do this, how much more the early Welsh professional *cyfarwyddiaid* must have been able to do it !

But if there is one thing on which most students of the Mabinogion are agreed it is that the plots of the *Four Branches*, to mention no others, are extraordinarily confused and incoherent,[65] so much so that there has been a wide divergence of opinion as to how some of these plots are to be explained and even what they really are. This has been the source of some very strange speculations and wild conjectures, which involve supposing that everyone and everything in the story can be or stand for almost everyone and everything else. It is not simply a question of extraneous motifs having been combined with others or inserted into them, or two or more separate main themes having been put together—after all, the present-day folktale tellers sometimes do this, and without wrecking the construction of the story. Rather it is that this has been done in such a way that the whole sense of the story has been violently distorted and even completely destroyed, as in the episode of the birth of Pryderi and the monstrous claw, so that it is sometimes scarcely possible now to discover what the original tale must have been. Nor is it solely a simple affair like the fact that in *Culhwch* the giant specifies a number of tasks to be performed which in the sequel never are performed, and that a number of other tasks are performed which he never specified—such things may be examples merely of bad memory, which may happen even to the best story-tellers on an off day. But with a good modern story-teller there is rarely any question as to how his story hangs together, and hence no books could be written disputing about how it is to be explained—unlike the *Four Branches*.

This is a problem which must be squarely faced; it is no use pretending that it does not exist, out of motives of piety or otherwise. Now, of recent years writers on the *Four Branches* have tended to stress the great story-telling skill of the final compiler of the tales as we have them. If this means that his plots are logical and lucid this is scarcely acceptable to anyone who asks himself how they hang together. If it means the skill and artistry of the compiler's prose style, of his actual language—as in fact it generally does—one must heartily agree; the language, the style, is indeed masterly for its ease, refinement, and limpidity, though I should like to stress once again that this does not of itself *necessarily* mean that the compiler cannot have been a folktale teller, since as I have already noted the traditional prose style used by good modern folktale tellers may be a matter of great artistry. However, I do not suggest that the compiler *was* a folktale teller; the tales are full of internal evidence that they acquired their present form in a courtly context. The life of the gentry, of the Welsh nobility and their courts with their customs and their formulae, are too intimately portrayed for it to be otherwise.[66] Granted, then, that the present form of the Mabinogion is the result of existing in a courtly setting, and that the stylistic skill of the final com-pilers suggests that they cannot have been mere clumsy botchers, why is it that the plots themselves are so disin-tegrated, at least in the case of the *Four Branches*, that an expert teller of folktales at the present day would reject them and indeed could scarcely handle them and transmit them?

The only explanation that I can see is this: these people were not themselves members of a corporate body of expert professional story-tellers with a long, firm, un-broken tradition of telling these very tales, in constant practice; and the fault lay in the character of the material they were trying to use. I suggest that the *Four Branches* and to some extent *Culhwch* represent very old tales which had gone out of fashion and were now only very ill-remembered. They must have passed through a stage of recitation by very inferior tellers—perhaps the pro-fessionals no longer practised them, and they lingered on only among non-professionals, much as Grimm's fairy-tales are often told to children by their parents from memory and—since the parents are not skilled story-tellers—the tale is apt to be badly corrupted. Then, I would envisage a courtly entertainer on the look-out for new material who 'revived' this old body of tales, which had been out of fashion so long that it was capable of being made fashionable and interesting once again. Perhaps these were vaguely known of as ancient classics now to be heard only on the lips of nursemaids and the like, and someone dug them out again and retold them. Incidentally, he inserted at this stage most of the various features which scholars have noted as obviously late; but he was not able clearly to restore the thread of the tales where this had been lost.

What the original tales of the *Four Branches*[67] which lay behind the suggested period of disuse and corruption were really like it is not easy to say; but it does seem evident that they were drawn from a very varied collection of sources. In the first place there are a number of international motifs and episodes like the Calumniated Wife, the riddle neither-in-a-house-nor-out-of-a-house, and all the others discussed in these lectures. I have already suggested various ways in which these immensely popular themes may have come to Wales. Secondly, there are motifs well known in Celtic tradition, and apparently only in Celtic tradition, such as the important episode of the human aid to hostile Otherworld chiefs which constitutes the first part of *Pwyll*. Such things may well go back to a very early period in the history of the Celtic peoples; at any rate it cannot be claimed, in the absence of good evidence, that they can only have reached Wales from Ireland. Thirdly, motifs are present which are indisputably of Irish origin, whether they got to Wales by oral transmission or whether they were adopted at a late stage from literary sources. Dr. Mac Cana has made a very good case in respect of some of these, in the tale of *Branwen*. Fourthly, there are a good many obvious interpolations of late, literary, semi-learned, and antiquarian origin, such as the triads and the historical and geographical associations of characters. These are likely to have been added by the courtly compilers of the tales in their final form.

Lastly, I would mention the mythological element. As I have already pointed out, the *Four Branches* were at one time regarded as primarily myths, tales about sun gods, fertility gods, and the rest, and capable of explanation if one could discover the rituals and beliefs about the gods supposed to be hidden under them. Such interpretations of the *international* popular tale have now long ceased to be accepted by serious folklorists, and rightly so, and I do not believe for a moment that any of the international motifs in the *Four Branches* represents a myth. Nevertheless, it is a fact that some of the names of characters are unquestionably those of ancient pagan Celtic gods and others probably are—Lleu is a good example, Don another, and all would agree that Mabon and his mother Modron are two others. It is not impossible that the tale that this boy was stolen from his mother when three nights old may represent some dimly remembered event in the myth of the Celtic Maponos, 'Boy-God', and his mother Matrona, 'Mother-Goddess'. The rest of the tale in *Culhwch* connected with Mabon, however, consists of international popular tale motifs, as I have shown, and it would be quite idle and indeed pernicious to attempt to account for these on the theory that they belong

to the myth or ritual of Maponos;[68] in fact even the story
of the stealing of the infant looks suspiciously like a
faded version of our friend ST. K. 2115 and following,
the Calumniated Wife. These scattered appearances of
purely Celtic divine figures and possible exiguous fragments of their myth are inheritances from the pagan
Celtic period which were used by the original composers
of the first tales, and round them there has been assembled
a mass of popular-tale motifs of very varied origin, international and non-international, just as King Arthur is a
figure of early history round whom gathered a quantity of
exactly the same kind of thing. By and large, however,
I think it is wise to regard mythological explanations of
even the non-international episodes in the Mabinogion
with cautious scepticism. Such interpretations can be
tailored to fit anything, and hence they are a favourite
device in the hands of the unscholarly. This is not to say
that they cannot be handled in a scholarly manner, but as
a common rule when a mythological explanation is fore-
shadowed one suspects that a speculation is likely to be
on its way, and probably a series of others erected on the
basis of that one. In any case, no theory involving the
supposition of a myth should even be advanced until
one has made sure that the motif one is studying is not an
international one.

Who was responsible for the final compilation of the
Four Branches and the rest as we have them I would not
attempt to say for certain, but I think it is likely that it
was done by literary and antiquarian-minded entertainers at the courts of the Welsh nobility, familiar with
Welsh lore and legend but not possessing any good
tradition of ancient oral story-telling in respect of these

particular tales. Perhaps in hunting for new material they discovered disjointed and ill-remembered versions of old superannuated classics, and brought them together and welded them into a fresh whole; these people being highly artistic and skilled prose stylists but not skilled *constructors* or *editors* of stories—hence the confusion in which their tales remain. They are perhaps to be regarded as antiquarian literary men rather than as courtly *cyfarwyddiaid*, and their work as the product of the study rather than the mead-hall, however much it may contain of the ancient traditional stories of the Welsh, of the Celts, and of early civilized man in general.

NOTES TO LECTURE IV

[1] M., pp. 30 f.

[2] BDL., pp. 16 ff.

[3] Cf. BP. ii, 87 ff.

[4] M., pp. 35 f.

[5] ST. K. 753.

[6] Masp., pp. 87 ff.

[7] M., pp. 39 f.

[8] ST. C. 611 and C. 611.1.

[9] For example, AT. 311, 312, 314, 710.

[10] R. Burton, *The Book of the Thousand Nights and a Night* (Benares ed., Burton Club, n.d.), i, 154–60.

[11] M., pp. 46 f.

[12] Cf. BP. ii, 40, n.2.

[13] M., pp. 49 ff.

[14] See E. S. Hartland, *English Folk and Fairy Tales* (London, 1894), p. 145. The supposed parallels in Irish mentioned by Gruffydd (Rh., p. 72) are too remote to constitute real parallels at all, and so is the one quoted from Rhys, *Celtic Folklore*, i, 124, by R. S. Loomis in his *Wales and the Arthurian Legend* (Cardiff, 1956), p. 103.

[15] GS., p. 218.

[16] *Math vab Mathonwy* (Cardiff, 1928). See also A. H. Krappe, *Balor with the Evil Eye* (New York, 1927), pp. 1–43.

[17] M., pp. 57 f.

[18] For some examples see E. S. Hartland, *The Science of Fairy Tales* (London, 1891), p. 50.

[19] A. W. Wade-Evans, VSB., pp. 68–70.

[20] M., pp. 69 ff.

[21] See Mary Williams, RC. xlvi (1929), 167 ff.

[22] See, for example, A. J. Carnoy, *Iranian Mythology* (The Mythology of All Races Series, vol. vi; Boston, 1917), p. 302; G. Huet, *Les Contes populaires* (Paris, 1923), p. 134.

[23] *trie diuide do didhnadh a broin.*

[24] BP. ii, 349 ff., particularly 362 ff.; KS. i, 445 ff.; Benfey, *Kleinere Schriften*, ii (Berlin, 1892), pp. iii, 156 ff.; and especially the study on the tale by J. de Vries, *Die Märchen von klugen Rätsellösern* (FFC., no. 73; Helsinki, 1928).

[25] Op. cit., pp. 17 ff.

[26] De Vries, op. cit., pp. 29 ff.

[27] Ibid., pp. 40 ff.

[28] Ibid., p. 180.

[29] TWH. iii, 40.

30 The motif is found in connexion with the birth of St. Bridget in the Irish *Life* of that saint; see W. Stokes, *Lives of Saints from the Book of Lismore* (*Anecdota Oxoniensia*, Oxford, 1890), p. 36, translation p. 184.

31 Op. cit., p. 177.

32 M., pp. 79 ff.

33 See the references given in ST.

34 BP. i, 42 ff.

35 Hermotimus, c. 73.

36 References, see TPC., p. 480.

37 See Norman Macleod, *Reminiscences of a Highland Parish* (London, 1867), p. 240; J. G. Campbell, SHS., p. 242; *Celtic Magazine*, xiii, 557 ff.

38 M., p. 199.

39 References, see BP. i, 462.

40 Cf. BP. i, 450.   41 iv, 9.

42 For example, Mary Williams, *Essai sur la composition du Roman Gallois de Peredur* (Paris, 1909), pp. 57 f.; R. S. Loomis, *Arthurian Tradition and Chrétien de Troyes* (New York, 1949), pp. 414 f.

43 H. Zimmer, *Keltische Studien*, ii (Berlin, 1884), 200 ff.

44 See Ifor Williams, *Lectures on Early Welsh Poetry* (Dublin, 1944), pp. 95 ff. Williams regards the Welsh story as at least as old as the ninth century in origin, though the extant texts are certainly centuries later. The oldest manuscript copy is sixteenth century.

45 For references see Cross, TPC., pp. 61 (B. 162.1) and 59 (B. 124.2).

46 See BP. i, 131 ff.

47 It is ST. E. 607.2; T. 511; &c.

48 For other examples see BP. i, 544.

49 Edited by F. Lot, *Nennius et l'Historia Brittonum* (Paris, 1934).

50 'Hen Chwedlau', *Transactions of the Honourable Society of Cymmrodorion*, 1946–7, pp. 28 ff.

51 Op. cit., c. 73.

52 Cf. Rhys, *Celtic Folklore*, i (Oxford, 1901), 142, the story of Carn March Arthur by Llyn Barfog near Aberdovey, with the hoofprint of Arthur's horse.

53 ST. A. 901.

54 *Historia Brittonum*, c. 32.

55 Cf. Krohn, FFC., no. 96, pp. 128 ff. Note the Irish version in the *Life of St. Mochua*, C. Plummer, *Vitae Sanctorum Hiberniae* (Oxford, 1910), ii, 188; and compare the Irish story of the pigs of Essach which could be killed every night and were whole again next morning if no bones were broken or gnawed, see ZCP. xii, 244.

56 Von Sydow, who has studied the tale in *Danske Studier*, 1910, pp. 91 ff., thinks it of Welsh origin, but the distribution suggests this is hardly likely.

57 See the discussion of this in my article in SEBC., pp. 350 ff.

58 See, for example, a very interesting note by M. Schlauch in JCS. i, 157 ff.

[59] See W. W. Heist, *The Fifteen Signs Before Doomsday* (Michigan State College, 1952).

[60] For further references see T. Batiouchkof, *Romania*, xx, 1 ff.; Wright, *The Latin Poems of Walter Mapes* (Camden Society, xvi, 1841), pp. 321 ff.; Sir Ifor Williams, *Transactions of the Honourable Society of Cymmrodorion*, 1913–14, p. 185; Henry Lewis, Thomas Roberts, and Ifor Williams, *Cywyddau Iolo Goch ac Eraill* (Bangor, 1925), p. 86; T. H. Parry-Williams, *Canu Rhydd Cynnar* (Cardiff, 1932), p. 295; M. Schlauch, JCS. i, 158; G. Dottin, RC. xxiii, 1 ff.

[61] See the writer's studies on this theme in the *Bulletin of the Board of Celtic Studies*, x (1940), 203 ff., and (especially) *Folk-Lore*, li (1940), 203 ff.

[62] *Folk-Lore*, xxvii (1916), 31 ff. Gruffydd's theories about the first part of *Pwyll* are thus irrelevant, besides being exceptionally unconvincing.

[63] In a confused and vague article in *Béaloideas*, vi (1936), 33 ff., J. T. Honti asserts the Irish *origin* of such international tales, but the assertion is not supported by any evidence, and it depends on preconceived ideas about Irish literature which do not correspond to the reality. Tales such as the Ring of Polycrates, &c., &c., cannot possibly have *originated* in Ireland.

[64] See p. 71.

[65] Cf. Rh., p. 4.

[66] It has been pointed out on p. 5 that folktale tellers are very vague about such matters.

[67] With *Culhwch* it is rather different; this is a comparatively well-preserved version of AT. 513A, though with an Arthurian setting and with parts of it (such as the Helpers) disproportionately expanded and with new episodes (such as the Boar Hunt) inserted. The source for *Culhwch* must have been a comparatively good one.

[68] Gruffydd believed that Rhiannon is an expression of Epona, a horse-goddess and goddess of Celtic cavalry regiments in the Roman army. Noting the motif (M., pp. 9 ff.) that it was impossible to catch up with her by galloping though she was only walking her horse, and that representations of Epona on altars, &c., never (according to him) show her horse galloping but only walking or trotting, he argued that the motif in *Pwyll* was part of the myth of Epona. One might point out that a walking or trotting horse is much easier to represent in a confined space than a galloping one; and one wonders what sort of goddess of cavalry was incapable of galloping! The motif occurs, of course, as a popular one in several other passages in Celtic literature not associated with Rhiannon at all (for one of these see MacCana, BDL., p. 40, n.2), and the supposed myth is a fantasy. See Rh., pp. 104 f.

General Index

A number in brackets is that of the page in the Lectures to which a reference in the Notes belongs.

Gabha an tSuic, 63.

Gaidoz, Henri, 39.

Gaster, M., 35 (20).

Gelert, 40, 90, 98 (92), 99.

Gerbold of Bayeux, St., 25.

Germanus, St., 117, 118.

Gerould, G. H., *The Ballad of Tradition*, 66 (44).

Gesta Romanorum, 31, 46.

Glaistig of Lianachan, the, 96.

Golden Ass, The, 80 f.

Gráinne, 110.

Grateful Animals, the, 35, 48, 79.

Grateful Dead Man, the, 23.

Gregory the Great, St., 25 f.

Grimm, the Brothers, 38, 45, 61, 67.

— *Kinder, und Hausmärchen*, 65 (38), 80, 115.

Gronw, 106 f.

Gruffydd, W. J., 1, 34 (6), 48, 49, 60, 66 (48), 84, 96 (77), 98 (90, 92), 99, 105, 131 (104), 133 (122, 124, 129).

— *Math vab Mathonwy*, 131 (105).

Gwawl, 85.

Gwefl son of Gwastad, 75.

Gwion Bach, 115 f.

Gwydion, 105.

Haavio, M., 35 (20).

Hackman, O., *Die Polyphemsage*, 35 (23).

Hafgan, 81, 82, 84, 85.

Haft Paikar, 20.

Halliday, W. R., *Indo-European Folktales and Greek Legend*, 96 (75).

Hand and Child, the, 90, 91, 92, 94, 98 (94), 99.

Hanes Taliesin, 115, 116.

Haroun al Rashid, 28.

Healing of Cian's Leg, the, 55.

Heist, W. W., *The Fifteen Signs before Doomsday*, 133 (120).

Helpers, the Magic, 73, 74, 75, 76, 79, 89, 92, 101, 133. *See* AT. 513 A and B.

Henwas the Winged, 74.

Herbert, the troubadour, 19.

Herodotus, 18, 25.

Hildebranslied, the, 71.

Hir Erwm and Hir Atrwm, 74.

Historia Brittonum, the, 117.

Historic-geographic method, the, 42 f.

Holmer, N., *The Irish Language in Rathlin Island*, 62.

Honti, J. T., 133.

Hull, Eleanor, 96 (77).

Hull, V., 96 (69).

Hyde, Douglas, 96 (77).

— *Leabhar Sgeulaigheachta*, 66 (61).

Indra, 113.

Irishmen in the Bags, the, 101 f.

Iron House, the, 100 f.

Jameson, R. D., *Three Lectures on Chinese Folklore*, 35 (25).

Jason, 73, 113.

Jatakas, the, 76.

Johannes de Alta Silva, 19.

Jones, Professor Thomas, vii, 77.

Judgement Day, (Welsh) poem on the, 120.

Kanjur, the, 18, 20.

Kathasaritsagara, the, 12, 19, 20, 69, 80, 90, 97.

Kentigern, St., 27, 68.

King and the Peasant's Son, The, 109; see AT. 921.

King John and the Abbot, 15 ff.

Kittredge, G. L., 88, 89, 90, 91, 95, 98, 99.

— 'Arthur and Gorlagon', 98, 99.

Köhler, R., 96 (71), 97 (84).

Koran, the, 28.

Kráka, 110.

Krappe, A. H., 97 (84).

Our Lady's Child, 88. *See* AT. 710.

Padmavati, 88.
Panchatantra, the, 20, 39, 46.
Parry, Principal T., vii.
Parry-Williams, Sir T. H., *Canu Rhydd Cynnar*, 133 (120).
Pentamerone, the, 17, 61, 80, 114.
Peredur, 114.
Perrault, Charles, *Contes de ma mere l'Oye*, 17.
Perseus and Danae, 105.
Perseus tale, *see* the Dragon Slayer.
Piacevole Notti, 35 (24), 59.
Polycrates, the Ring of, 25 ff., 35, 44, 68.
Polygenesis, 37, 41, 44, 75, 117.
Polyphemus, 23.
Potiphar's Wife, 26.
Potter, M. A., Sohrab and Rustem, 96 (71).
Prince whose Wishes came True, the, 88.
Princess and the Riddles, the, 63.
Pryderi, 87, 99 (94), 104, 105.
Pwyll, 81, 82, 83, 84, 85, 97.
Pwyll, 81, 82, 83, 84, 85, 90, 91, 93, 97, 99, 122, 127, 133.

Ragnar Lodbrok, saga of, 110, 112.
Ranke, K., 34 (14), 66 (63).
Raoul le Tourtier, 82, 83.
'Re-birth, the Celtic doctrine of', 116.
Red Book of Hergest, the, 19, 39, 83.
Regin, 116.
Rhampsinitus, 18, 19.
Rhiannon, 85, 86, 87, 88, 92, 93, 94, 95, 99 (94), 104, 133.
Rhys, Sir John, 39, 91, 93, 131 (104), 132 (117).
Richard Middleton, 50.

Rich Man and his Son-in-law, the, 70.
Ring of Polycrates, the, *see* Polycrates, the Ring of.
Ripple theory, the, 42 f.
Robin Hood, 4.
Rohaka, 110, 111, 113.
Roman Empire, 46, 67, 74.

Saif al-Muluk, 84.
Saintyves, Pierre, 35, 41.
Sakuntala, 27.
Samson and Delilah, 107.
Sayers, Peig, frontispiece, v, 7, 30, 54, 59, 63.
Sceolang, 89, 92.
Schick, J., *Corpus Hamleticum*, 96 (70).
Schlauch, M., 96 (70), 132 (120), 133 (120).
— *Chaucer's Constance*, 98 (87).
School of Scottish Studies, the, 31, 34 (11), 35, 96.
Search for the Lost Husband, the, 79 f.
Serglige Conculainn, 122.
Seven Sages of Rome, The, 19, 39.
Shah Nameh, the, 71.
Sigurd, 115 f.
Sir Amadas, 35 (24).
Six go through the World, 72, 101. *See* AT. 513A.
Smith Outwits the Devil, The, 85.
Snow White, 32, 61, 114.
Sohrab and Rustem, 71.
Solomon, King, 28.
Somadeva, 12.
Sons of the King and the Smith, The, 109.
Spanish galleon at Tobermory, the, 114.
Sringabhuja, 12, 48, 80.
Straparola, see *Piacevole Notti*.
Sugn son of Sugnedydd, 75.

Index of AT. Numbers

Index of ST. Numbers

PRINTED IN GREAT BRITAIN
AT THE UNIVERSITY PRESS, OXFORD
BY VIVIAN RIDLER
PRINTER TO THE UNIVERSITY